REFERENCE

The Page and The Fire
СТРАНИЦА И ОГОНЬ

The Page and The Fire

С Т Р А Н И Ц А И О Г О Н Ь

A COLLECTION OF POEMS BY RUSSIAN POETS ON RUSSIAN POETS

❧

Selected, translated and introduced by

Peter Oram

Arc
PUBLICATIONS
2007

Published by Arc Publications,
Nanholme Mill, Shaw Wood Road
Todmorden OL14 6DA, UK

Design by Tony Ward
Printed by Biddles Ltd.,
King's Lynn, Norfolk, UK

ISBN-13: 978 1904614 42 5 pbk
ISBN-13: 978 1904614 67 8 hbk

ACKNOWLEDGMENTS

The poems in Russian are reproduced by kind permission of the
FTM Agency Ltd., Moscow.

Peter Oram's translations of 'Dislocated...' by Tsvetaeva, 'Verses
for Blok' by Pasternak and 'Yesenin' by Severyanin first ap-
peared in *The Amsterdam Review*; his translations of Severyanin's
poems on Mayakovsky, Pasternak, Gumilev, Blok, Akhmatova
and Tsvetaeva first appeared in *Poetry Salzburg Review*.

Cover painting:
'Fantasy' by
Kuzma Petrov-Vodkin (c. 1917)

The publishers acknowledge financial assistance
from ACE Yorkshire

LOTTERY FUNDED

Arc Publications Translations Series
Translations Editor: Jean Boase-Beier

i.m. Phil Malleson
(1946-2007)
in the hope that he might have
appreciated these

CONTENTS

The early years of the twentieth century saw a remarkable flourishing in the life of Russian poetry. The so-called Symbolist movement had reached a kind of culmination with Alexander Blok, but out of its embers there arose a number of energetic poet-groups, each with its own bright stars and lesser satellites, its own principles and manifestos, its own self-important label. Acmeism, Futurism, Ego-Futurism, the Centrifuge... if one thing was common to these widely-differing movements it was an urge to put aside the deliberate obscurity, the ambiguity and the mystic pretensions that had become the poetic vogue, and replace them with a new linguistic honesty and directness. These cliques would, though, be of little interest to us today had they not fostered the early development of poets of such stature as Akhmatova, Mandelstam, Mayakovsky or Pasternak.

At a time in Russian history like no other, with its tumultuous changes on the largest scale, and its high ideals that would soon dissolve into disillusion, repression and terror, it's perhaps not surprising that the various practitioners of what is essentially a solitary art should be particularly aware of one another's existence and activities, and that there should be a mutual nurturing of common bonds. This may at least partly explain the unusually high incidence, in the works of the major figures, of poems to, about, or in memory of other poets of the time. It is a selection of such verse that this book presents, together with some examples of the same tradition as it continues through the subsequent decades. It is by no means exhaustive, and in many cases a poem included is only one of a whole cycle of poems by the same writer to the same recipient.

Such a monothematic anthology might prove a tedious read, were it not for the first-rank quality of the poets and their highly-differentiated voices. Compare the almost classical, yet thoroughly modern, purity of Mandelstam with, say, the electric vitality of Tsvetaeva, Mayakovsky's thundering rhythms and colloquialisms with Pasternak's restrained quatrains and unexpected metaphors, or Severyanin's pitiless irreverence with Akhmatova's simple, acutely sensitive profundity. Where there are a number of items addressed to one poet, it is illuminating to witness the various perceptions as they contrast with, or corroborate, one another and so build up a three-dimensional picture of the individual concerned. Several of

9

the examples are *in memoriam,* and it is a tragic fact that many of these lives were to end in suicide, execution, or a wretched death in exile. Nevertheless, I believe that this little collection reflects and confirms an inextinguishable vitality in Russian poetic life and the unshakeable faith of the Russian poet in the written word.

A NOTE ON THE TRANSLATIONS

It is generally taken for granted that a true and complete translation of poetry is impossible. And quite rightly so. Any pair of languages is, in the words of Borges, 'not a set of interchangeable synonyms but two possible ways of ordering reality', and even such a simple word as *tree* says something different to us than *Baum* says to a German, or *árbol* to a Spaniard. And even if one could communicate the literal sense of each word, what of its connotations, associations, and the particular resonance in both the ear and the heart of its unique blend of sounds? When we call into consideration the numerous other elements – rhythm, metre, rhyme, alliteration and assonance, wordplays and double meanings, and everything else that contributes to a poem's individual essence – then the translator's task does indeed become not only impossible but also highly presumptuous.

In Russian, the problems are compounded in many ways. The sound-patterns and word-structures of the language are supremely versatile and allow the poet to play with the language in a way that is unimaginable for us. Furthermore, a Russian word may have half a dozen or more syllables, yet only one main stress, and thus the Russian equivalent of the ten-syllable pentameter has lightness, spring and a forward dynamic, whereas the English iambics can plod dreadfully if they are not handled with great care – a dangerous trap for the translator. Other factors are the absence of the definite and indefinite article in Russian, and of the present tense of the verb 'to be', and the limited number of verb-tenses in general. In English, such things often have to be pinned down, and indeed the image of a colourful butterfly impaled on a pin is not far off the mark for much translation of Russian poetry.

In the light of the above, I've preferred to be modest in my ambitions, accepting that I can't do the impossible. I've done my best to convey the literal meaning of each poem as accurately as I'm able, in clear and intelligible contemporary English. This is the least one must do. Beyond this, I've reproduced, where it didn't require forcing the issue on principle, the general structure: line count, verse-form, rhyme patterns – and also meter, though this latter especially can never truly reflect or do justice to the original. Finally, I have worked and reworked each translation as I would a poem of my own, listening to its voice and responding to it, fine-tuning it, until I felt that it 'spoke', and that it could stand upon its own as a humble, yet sincere, homage to the original.

It was never my intention to recreate these poems in my own image as, for example, Don Paterson has done with Machado in *The Eyes*, where his own poetic identity is at least as present as that of the poet he translates (which in no way implies a deprecation of his fine work). I've tried to keep my own identity well in the background, and although these translations can never, even to a small extent, assume the status of the originals, I'd like to hope that they might be used by those who have little or no knowledge of Russian yet wish to find a way to 'meet' the Russian poets of the twentieth century. I'd like them to serve as mirrors in which one may, by looking carefully, see the originals dimly reflected.

*

This book would not have been possible without the extremely generous help and support of Anastasia Nikolaevna, who went through my work with a fine-tooth comb, putting me straight on numerous *faux pas* and also supplying several useful points of information, and Hanna Strom, who provided many illuminating insights into the poems and their allusions and undertones.

My warm thanks also go to Alex Barr who, via a protracted yet invigorating e-mail correspondence, lent his perceptively critical eye to the developing versions of each poem.

Peter Oram

11

The Page and The Fire

АЛЕКСАНДРУ БЛОКУ

Я пришла к поэту в гости.
Ровно полдень. Воскресенье.
Тихо и комнате просторной,
А за окнами мороз

И малиновое солнце
Над лохматым сизым дымом...
Как хозяин молчаливый
Ясно смотрит на меня!

У него глаза такие,
Что запомнить каждый должен;
Мне же лучше, осторожной,
В них и вовсе не глядеть.

Но запомнится беседа,
Дымный полдень, воскресенье,
В доме сером и высоком
У морских ворот Невы.

(Анна Ахматова)

I've come to visit the poet.
It's exactly midday. Sunday.
The room is quiet and spacious.
Outside the windows: frost,

and a raspberry-coloured sun
over shreds of bluish smoke…
My host observes me, silent.
Such a bright, unswerving gaze!

His are the kind of eyes
you can't help but remember.
I'd think I'd better be careful,
not look into them at all.

But I won't forget what was spoken
on a smoky midday, a Sunday,
in the high grey house where the Neva
opens its gates to the sea.

(Anna Akhmatova)

СТИХИ К БЛОКУ

Имя твое – птица в руке,
Имя твое – льдинка на языке.
Одно-единственное движенье губ.
Имя твое – пять букв.
Мячик, пойманный на лету,
Серебряный бубенец во рту.

Камень, кинутый в тихий пруд,
Всхлипнет так, как тебя зовут.
В легком щелканье ночных копыт
Громкое имя твое гремит.
И назовет его нам в висок
Звонко щелкающий курок.

Имя твое – ах, нельзя!
Имя твое – поцелуй в глаза,
В нежную стужу недвижных век.
Имя твое – поцелуй в снег.
Ключевой, ледяной, голубой глоток.
С именем твоим – сон глубок.

(Марина Цветаева, 1916)

16

VERSES FOR BLOK

Your name's a bird in the hand,
a chip of ice on the tongue,
a single flip of the lips,
a five-letter hieroglyph,
a flying ball caught in the palm,
a silver bell pressed on the gum.

A stone tossed into a quiet pond
makes your name's soft, sobbing sound;
resonant, in the muffled beating
of hooves at night it keeps repeating,
and is heard again in the hollow knock
of a pistol held to the head and cocked.

Your name – an impossible cry!
Your name – a kiss on the eye,
on the motionless eyelid's delicate frost,
the sound that a snowflake makes when kissed,
a gulp of spring water, icy, blue, deep…
at the sound of your name – profoundest sleep.

(Marina Tsvetaeva, 1916)

АННЕ АХМАТОВОЙ

"Красота страшна" – Вам скажут, –
Вы накинете лениво
Шаль испанскую на плечи,
Красный розан – в волосах.

"Красота проста" – Вам скажут, –
Пестрой шалью неумело
Вы укроете ребенка,
Красный розан – на полу.

Но, рассеянно внимая
Всем словам, кругом звучащим,
Вы задумаетесь грустно
И твердите про себя:

"Не страшна и не проста я;
Я не так страшна, чтоб просто
Убивать; не так проста я,
Чтоб не знать, как жизнь страшна."

(Александр Блок, 1913)

TO ANNA AKHMATOVA

"Beauty's terrifying", they'll say.
With an idle move, you throw
the Spanish shawl around your shoulders.
A red rose nestles in your hair.

"Beauty's simple", so they'll say.
Clumsily, you try to calm
the child beneath your coloured shawl.
The red rose lies upon the floor.

But, listening absentmindedly
to all these words that float around,
you'll lose yourself in mournful thoughts,
and keep repeating to yourself:

"I'm neither simple nor terrible.
Not so terrible that I'd simply
go out and kill. And not so simple
that I don't know the terror of living."

(Alexander Blok, 1913)

БОРИС ПАСТЕРНАК
   (поэт)

Он, сам себя сравнивший с конским глазом,
Косится, смотрит, видит, узнает,
И вот уже расплавленным алмазом
Сияют лужи, изнывает лед.

В лиловой мгле покоятся задворки,
Платформы, бревна, листья, облака.
Свист паровоза, хруст арбузной корки,
В душистой лайке робкая рука.

Звенит, гремит, скрежещет, бьет прибоем
И вдруг притихнет, – это значит, он
Пугливо пробирается по хвоям,
Чтоб не спугнуть пространства чуткий сон.

И это значит, он считает зерна
В пустых колосьях, это значит, он
К плите дарьяльской, проклятой и черной,
Опять пришел с каких-то похорон.

И снова жжет московская истома.
Звенит вдали смертельный бубенец…
Кто заблудился в двух шагах от дома,
Где снег по пояс и всему конец.

За то, что дым сравнил с Лаокооном,
Кладбищенский воспел чертополох,
За то, что мир наполнил новым звоном
В пространстве новом отраженных строф, –

Он награжден каким-то вечным детством,
Той щедростью и зоркостью светил,
И вся земля была его наследством,
А он ее со всеми разделил.

(Анна Ахматова, 1936)

BORIS PASTERNAK
   ('Poet')

He who compared himself to a horse's eye
swivels his gaze, and looks, and sees – and knows,
and all at once the helpless ice surrenders,
like molten diamond puddle-water glows.

In the hazy lilac light, half-sleeping,
lie railway platforms, log-piles, clouds and leaves.
The crack of melon rind, an engine's shrieking.
Shy hands slip into perfumed kidskin gloves.

A ringing, scuffling, scraping, wave-like swishing,
then sudden quiet. This means he's on his way,
but cautiously, afraid to wake by crashing
between the pines the lightly dreaming day.

Or else it means perhaps that he's been counting
the grains in dry and barren ears of corn,
or after one more funeral is returning
to Daryal's Gorge, the black, accursed stone.

Somewhere far away a death bell's tolling.
He burns with Moscow's weariness once more…
Who's this who's lost his way, is blindly trawling
through waist-deep snow two yards from his front door?

Because he likened curling smoke to Laocoön,
because he sung of thistles in the graveyards,
because he filled the world with unknown sounds
that echoed back from spaces undiscovered

he's now repaid with childhood eternal,
as luminous and selfless as the stars,
and the whole world is his inheritance.
A world he freely shares with all of us.

(Anna Akhmatova, 1936)

21

МАРИНЕ ЦВЕТАЕВОЙ

Ты вправе, вывернув карман,
сказать: ищите, ройтесь, шарьте.
Мне все равно, чем сыр туман.
Любая быль – как утро в марте.

Деревья в мягких армяках
Стоят в грунту из гумигута,
Хотя ветвям наверняка
Невмоготу среди закута.

Роса бросает ветки в дрожь,
Струясь, как шерсть на мериносе,
Роса бежит, тряся, как еж,
Сухой копной у переносья.

Мне все равно, чей разговор
Ловлю, плывущий ниоткуда.
Любая быль – как вешний двор,
когда он дымкою окутан.

Мне все равно, какой фасон
сужден при мне покрою платьев.
Любую быль сметут как сон,
Поэта в ней законопатив.

Клубясь во много рукавов,
Он двинется, подобно дыму,
Из дыр эпохи роковой
В иной тупик непроходимый.

Он вырвется, курясь, из прорв
Судеб, расплющенных в лепеху,
И внуки скажут, как про торф:
Горит такого-то эпоха.

(Борис Пастернак, 1928)

You've a right, as you turn your pockets out,
to say: dig in, then, rummage, search.
I don't care why the fog's so wet –
any event's just a morning in March.

In their soft peasant coats the trees
stand in the sticky, yellow earth,
their branches, though, resenting these
thick layers that they're covered with.

The dew is trembling on the twigs
and, gleaming like merino fleece,
goes trickling down and makes them shake
like a hedgehog shakes his crop of spears.

I don't care whose conversation
I catch, floating in from anywhere –
any event's just a courtyard in spring
when a veil of haze is on the air.

I don't care what fad of the day
prescribes what kind of clothes will do.
All events are swept away
like dreams, and the poet's entangled too.

Swirling, branching at every stage,
he advances like a cloud of smoke,
slips through gaps in a fateful age
into some hopeless *cul-de-sac*.

At last, smouldering, he breaks out
through layers of fate-crushed souls, returns,
and the grandchildren say, as they'd say of peat:
that's how the age of so-and-so burns!

(Boris Pasternak, 1928)

23

АХМАТОВОЙ

Кем полосынька твоя
Нынче выжнется?
Чернокосынька моя,
Чернокнижница!

Дни полночные твои,
Век твой таборный…
Все работнички твои
Разом забраны.

Где сподручники твои,
Те сподвижнички?
Белорученька моя,
Чернокнижница!

Не загладить тех могил
Слезой, славою.
Один заживо ходил —
Как удавленный.

Другой к стеночке пошел
Искать прибыли.
(И гордец же был — сокол!)
Разом выбыли.

Высоко твои братья!
Не докличешься!
Яснооконька моя,
Чернокнижница!

А из тучи-то (хвала —
Диво дивное!)
Соколиная стрела,
Голубиная…

TO ANNA AKHMATOVA

Must your acre of land
now be reaperless?
My little black-haired one,
my sorceress!

Your midnight days...
your vagabond age...
all of your labourers
thrown in a cage!

Where are your allies,
your comrades-in-arms?
My little white-handed one,
weaver of charms!

Neither fame nor lament
can a burial revoke.
One, while still living,
went round as if choked.

The other one sought out
the wall, and he won
his reward, the proud falcon
Now both men are gone.

They're too high up, your brothers!
They can't hear your distress,
my little bright-eyed one,
my sorceress!

But out of the clouds
(praise! – all wonders above!)
flies an arrow – a falcon!
an arrow – a dove!

25

Знать, в два перышка тебе
пишут тамотка,
Знать, уж вскорости тебе
Выйдет грамотка:

– Будет крылышки трепать
О булыжники!
Чернокрылонька моя!
Чернокнижница!

(Марина Цветаева, 1921)

Maybe even out there
quills are writing away,
and your summons too
may turn up any day

and your wings will be dragged
over cobblestones – yes!
My little black-winged one,
my sorceress!

(Marina Tsvetaeva, 1921)

ПОЗДНИЙ ОТВЕТ

Белорученька моя,
чернокнижница...
                    М.Ц.

Невидимка, двойник, пересмешник...
Что ты прячешься в черных кустах? –
То забьешься в дырявый скворешник,
То блеснешь на погибших крестах,
То кричишь из Маринкиной башни:
"Я сегодня вернулась домой,
полюбуйтесь, родимые пашни,
Что за это случилось со мной.
Поглотила любимых пучина,
И разграблен родительский дом".

Мы сегодня с тобою, Марина,
По столице полночной идем.
А за нами таких миллионы
И безмолвнее шествия нет...
А вокруг погребальные звоны
Да московские хриплые стоны
Вьюги, наш заметающей след.

(Анна Ахматова, 1940)

FINAL REPLY
[to Marina Tsvetaeva]
My little white-handed one,
Weaver of charms…
(Tsvetaeva)

Invisible double with the voice that mocks!
Why do you hide away in blackened bushes?
You thrash about in your old nesting-box,
flit in and out among the broken crosses –
or from your private tower-room you cry:
"I've come back to the place that's meant to be
my home: familiar fields, cast your eye
this way, and look at what's become of me:
my loved ones swallowed up by the abyss,
my childhood dwelling desecrated, plundered…"

This midnight, through the great metropolis
go you and I, Marina, and behind us
a million others like us. No procession
ever was more silent. Yet the space is
ringing with the death bells' dull intoning
and all around us Moscow's blizzard, groaning
hoarse-throated as it covers up our traces.

(Anna Akhmatova, 1940)

РАС-СТОЯНИЕ...

Б. Пастернаку

Рас – стояние: версты, мили...
Нас рас – ставили, рас – садили,
Чтобы тихо себя вели,
По двум разным концам земли.

Рас – стояние: версты, дали...
Нас расклеили, распаяли,
В две руки развели, распяв,
И не знали, что это – сплав

Вдохновенний и сухожилий...
Не рассорили – рассорили,
Расслоили...
               Стена да ров.
Расселили нас, как орлов-

Заговорщиков: версты, дали...
Не расстроили – растеряли.
По трущобам земных широт
Рассовали нас как сирот.

Который уж – ну который – март?!
Разбили нас – как колоду карт!

(Марина Цветаева, 1925)

30

DIS-LOCATED...

To Boris Pasternak

Dis-located: separated
by miles, dis-joined, dis-seminated
so each stay quietly in his place
at either end of the planet's face.

Distances divide, exclude us.
They've dis-welded and dis-glued us.
Despatched, disposed of, dis-inclusion –
they never knew that this meant fusion

of elbow-grease and inspiration:
not dissonance, yet dissipation,
dissociation...
                Ditch and wall put there
to disconnect us like a pair

of scheming eagles. Miles that faced us!
They didn't destroy us, but displaced us:
through endless thickets, thorny, wild
they dragged us like an orphan child.

What day was it – in March? – think hard! –
dispersed – dealt out like a deck of cards!

(Marina Tsvetaeva, 1925)

31

ВЕТЕР
   [Блоку]

Кому быть живым и хвалимым,
Кто должен быть мертв и хулим,
Известно у нас подхалимам
Влиятельным только одним.

Не знал бы никто, может статься,
В почете ли Пушкин иль нет,
Без докторских их диссертаций,
На все проливающих свет.

Но Блок, слава Богу, иная,
Иная, по счастью, статья.
Он к нам не спускался с Синая,
Нас не принимал в сыновья.

Прославленный не по программе
И вечный вне школ и систем,
Он не изготовлен руками
И нам не навязан никем.

   (Борис Пастернак)

THE WIND
[To Blok]

Who deserves immortal glories,
who's written off without a glance
we only know from learned stories
by influential sycophants.

You might not know if it was right
to trust in Pushkin's reputation
without the scrutinizing light
of Ph.D and dissertation.

Thank God, though, when we turn to Blok,
he's altogether different – is
no Moses come down from the rock
to lecture us like kids of his.

His fame's not programmed, no, he stands
eternal, from systems, schools remote,
he wasn't formed by idle hands
or forcibly thrust down our throat.

(Boris Pasternak)

Б. АХМАДУЛИНОЙ

Нас много. Нас может быть четверо.
Несемся в машине как черти.
Оранжеволоса шоферша.
И куртка по локоть – для форса.

Ах, Белка, лихач катастрофный,
нездешняя ангел на вид,
люблю твой фарфоровый профль,
как белая лампа горит!

В аду в сковородки долдонят
и вышлют к воротам патруль,
когда на предельном спидометре
ты куришь, отбросивши руль.

Люблю, когда выжав педаль,
хрустально, как тексты в хорале,
ты скажешь: "какая печаль!
Права у меня отобрали…

Понимаешь, пришили превышение скорости
в возбужденном состоянии…
А шла я вроде нормально…"

Не порть себе, Белочка, печень.
Сержант нас, конечно, мудрей,
но нет твоей скорости певчей
в коробке его скоростей.

Обязанности поэта
нестись, позабыв ОРУД,
брать звуки со скоростью света,
как ангелы в небе поют.

There were loads of us. Well – about four.
The car was careering pell-mell.
And with us the orange-haired driver,
sleeves rolled up, stylish as hell.

Oh Belka, most reckless of road-hogs!
What an outlandish, angelic sight!
I adore your porcelain profile
like a lamp that's brilliantly white.

In Hades they fire up the griddle
and send a patrol to the gates
when your speedo's gone way past the middle
and you recklessly roll cigarettes.

I love it when, racing still faster,
in a voice clear as crystal you say:
"Oh dear, it's such a disaster.
They've taken my licence away...

...You see, they booked me for breaking the speed limit
while in a state of emotional excitement, but
I was just driving normally..."

Oh Belka, don't stress out your liver.
Our dear sergeant keeps getting it wrong,
but the speed of his gearbox, however,
just can't match the speed of your song.

It's a poet's first duty, in spite
of the traffic restrictions to fly,
bringing sound at the speed of light
like the angels that sing in the sky.

За эти года световые
пускай мы исчезнем, лучась,
пусть некому приз получать.
Мы выжали скорость впервые.

Жми, Белка, божественный кореш!
И пусть не собрать нам костей.
Да здравствует певчая скорость,
убийственнейшая из скоростей!

Что нам впереди предначертано?
Нас мало. Нас может быть четверо.
Мы мчимся –
а ты божество!
И все-таки нас большинство.

(Андрей Вознесенский, 1963)

And though after travelling light years
we may in a flash disappear,
though we may not collect any prizes –
it was we who first got into gear.

So Bel, press the celestial lever,
though our bones find nowhere to rest.
Long live the song-gear, forever!
Of all gears the deadliest!

What's engraved in the future to meet us?
There are few of us. Well – about four.
But we race on
        – and since you're a goddess,
the majority's ours for sure.

(Andrey Vosnesensky, 1963)

ОБ ОСИПЕ МАНДЕЛЬШТАМЕ

В том времени, где злодей –
лишь заурядный житель улиц,
как грозно хрупок иудей,
в ком Русь и музыка очнулись.

Вступленые: ломкий силуэт,
повинный в грациозном форсе.
Начало века. Младость лет.
Сырое лето в Гельсингфорсе.

Та – Бог иль барышня? Мольба –
чрез сотни верст любви нечеткой.
Любуется! И гений лба
застенчиво завешен челкой.

Но век желает пировать!
Измученный, он ждет предлога –
и Петербургу Петроград
оставит лишь предсмертье Блока.

Знал и сказал, что будет знак
и век падет ему на плечи.
Что может он? Он нищ и наг
пред чудом им свершенной речи.

Гортань, затеявшая речь
неслыханную, – так открыта.
Довольно, чтоб ее пресечь,
и меньшего усердья быта.

Ему – особенный почет,
двоякое злорадство небо:
певец, снабженный кляпом в рот,
и лакомка, лишенный хлеба.

In those days when a villain was
just another neighbour upon the block,
how menacing that fragile Jew
in whom Russia and music re-awoke.

Prelude: a silhouette, delicate
yet guilty of a graceful swagger.
The youthful years of a new century.
Helsinki, that rainy summer.

That God? Or girl? – a prayer over miles
and miles for some love vague and strange.
Just think of it! But the genius shyly
hides himself behind his fringe.

The new age longs to celebrate
itself, and waits exhausted for
an excuse, yet Petrograd retains
of Petersburg Blok's death, nothing more.

He knew, and said, there'd be a sign:
the age will break his back. What choice
has he? – naked, destitute, and faced
with the wonder of his awakening voice.

His larynx, probing forms of speech
unheard of, opens, is released.
The lesser chores of daily life
should be enough to silence it.

Yet as a special treat for him
a double sadism's applied:
a gourmet, he's deprived of bread,
a troubadour, his mouth is tied.

Из мемуаров: "Мандельштам
любил пирожные". Я рада
узнать об этом. Но дышать —
не хочется, да и не надо.

Так, значит, пребывать творцом,
за спину заломивши руки,
и безымянным мертвецом
всё ж недостаточно для муки?

И в смерти надо знать беду
той, не утихшей ни однажды,
беспечной, выжившей в аду,
неутолимой детской жажды?

В моем кошмаре, в том раю,
где жив он, где его я прячу,
он сыт! И я его кормлю
огромной сладостью! И плачу!

(Белла Ахмадулина, 1967)

A memoir entry: "Mandelstam
loved cakes". I'm very glad to read
of this. But when it comes to breathing
he has no longer wish nor need.

Does that mean, to leave the artist with
a corpse in anonymity
and broken hands tied at his back
is insufficient agony?

In death, must one know that distress
that there is no way of relieving –
to live in hell, in endlessness,
with an unquenchable childish craving?

In my nightmares, in that Eden
in which he lives, in which I keep him
his hunger's stilled – yet I force-feed him
huge lumps of cake, and I am weeping.

(Bella Akhmadulina, 1967)

41

АХМАТОВА

Вполоборота, о печаль,
На равнодушных поглядела.
Спадая с плеч, окаменела
Ложноклассическая шаль.

Зловещий голос – горький хмель –
Души расковывает недра:
Так – негодующая Федра –
Стояла некогда Рашель.

(Осип Мандельштам, 1914)

Half-turning, Sorrow, you looked upon
the hosts of the indifferent, while
a shawl, mock-classical in style,
slipped from your shoulders, turned to stone.

A voice, ill-omened, bitter-brewed
unlocks the caverns of the soul.
Thus, years ago, when in the rôle
of outraged Phaedra, Rachel stood.

(Ossip Mandelstam, 1914)

ВОРОНЕЖ

И город весь стоит оледенелый.
Как под стеклом деревья, стены, снег.
По хрусталям я прохожу несмело.
Узорных санок так неверен бег.
А над Петром воронежским – вороны,
Да тополя, и свод светло-зеленый,
Размытый, мутный, в солнечной пыли,
И куликовской битвой веют склоны
Могучей, победительной земли.
И тополя, как сдвинутые чаши,
Над нами сразу зазвенят сильней,
Как будто пьют за ликованье наши
На брачном пире тысячи гостей.

А в комнате опального поэта
Дежурят страх и Муза в свой черед.
И ночь идет,
Которая не ведает рассвета.

(Анна Ахматова)

VORONEZH
[to Ossip Mandelstam]

All the town's gripped in an icy fist.
Trees and walls and snow are set in glass.
I pick my timid way across the crystal.
Unsteadily the painted sledges pass.
Flocks of crows above St. Peter's, wheeling.
The dome amongst the poplars, green and pale in
subdued and dusty winter sunlight, and
echoes of ancient battles that come stealing
out across the proud, victorious land.
All of a sudden, overhead, the poplars
rattle, like glasses ringing in a toast,
as if a thousand guests were raising tumblers
to celebrate the marriage of their host.

But back in the banished poet's little room
the Muse and Fear take turns to keep
a watch. And night creeps in,
a night so deep its dawn will never come.

(Anna Akhmatova)

* * *

В разноголосице девического хора
Все церкви нежные поют на голос свой,
И в дугах каменных Успенского собора
Мне брови чудятся, высокие, дугой.

И с укрепленного архангелами вала
Я город озирал на чудной высоте.
В стенах Акрополая печаль меня снедала
По русском имени и русской красоте.

Не диво ль дивное, что вертоград нам снится
Где реют голуби в горячей синеве,
Что православные крюки поет черница:
Успенье нежное – Флоренция в Москве.

И пятиглавые московские соборы
С их итальянскою и русскою душой
Напоминают мне явление Авроры,
Но с русским именем и в шубке меховой.

(Осип Мандельштам, 1916)

[For Marina Tsvetaeva]

Polyphonous, like choirs of maidens, sing
each with its own voice the gentle churches,
and where Uspenski's stone-built arches swing,
I see the rising curve of eyebrows' arches.

And from these ramparts, which archangels forged,
I looked out from on high across the city.
I stood on the wall of an Acropolis, ravaged
by grief for a Russian name and Russian beauty.

No wonder that those gardens haunt our dreams
where ring-doves flutter round in the blue heat.
A nun is chanting, orthodox, her neumes.
Florence in Moscow – such Ascension's sweet!

The fivefold form of Moscow's great cathedrals
with half-Italian and half-Russian soul
awakes in me the coming of Aurora,
with a Russian name and wrapped in a fur stole.

(Ossip Mandelstam, 1916)

[Осипу Мандельштаму]

Никто ничего не отнял –
Мне сладостно, что мы врозь!
Целую вас через сотни
Разъединяющих верст.

Я знаю: наш дар – неравен.
Мой голос впервые – тих.
Что вам, молодой Державин,
Мой невоспитанный стих!

На страшный полет крещу вас:
– Лети, молодой орел!
Ты солнце стерпел, не щурясь, –
Юный ли взгляд мой тяжел?

Нежней и бесповоротней
Никто не глядел вам вслед…
Целую вас – через сотни
Разъединяющих лет.

(Марина Цветаева, 12 февраля, 1916)

[To Ossip Mandelstam]

Nothing's been taken away!
We're apart – I'm delighted at this!
Across the hundreds of miles
that divide us, I send you my kiss.

Our gifts, I know, are unequal.
For the first time my voice is still.
What, my young Dershavin, do
you make of my doggerel?

For your terrible flight I baptise you –
young eagle, it's time to take wing!
You endured the sun without blinking,
but my gaze – that's a different thing!

None ever watched your departure
more tenderly than this
or more finally. Across hundreds
of summers, I send you my kiss.

(Marina Tsvetaeva, 12 February 1916)

МАЯКОВСКОМУ

Превыше крестов и труб,
Крещенный в огне и дыме,
Архангел-тяжелоступ –
Здорово, в веках Владимир!

Он возчик, и он же конь,
Он прихоть, и он же право.
Вдохнул, поплевал в ладонь
– Держись, ломовая слава!

Певец площадных чудес –
Здорово, гордец чумазый,
Что камнем – тяжеловес
Избрал, не прельстясь алмазом.

Здорово, булыжный гром!
Зевнул, козырнул – и снова
Оглоблей гребет – крылом
Архангела ломового.

(Марина Цветаева, 18 сентября 1921)

TO MAYAKOVSKY

Beyond the chimneys and steeples,
baptised by smoke and flame,
stamping-footed archangel,
down the decades I call your name!

Rock-steady or change-at-a-whim!
Coachman and stallion in one!
He snorts and spits into his palm –
chariot of glory, hold on!

Singer of city-square wonders,
I salute that arrogant tone
that rejected the brilliant diamond
for the sake of the ponderous stone.

I salute you, cobblestone-thunderer!
– see, he yawns, gives a wave, then he swings
himself back into harness, back under
the shafts, his archangelic wings.

(Marina Tsvetaeva, 18 September 1921)

МАЯКОВСКИЙ

Саженным – в нем посаженным – стихам
Сбыт находя в бродяжьем околотке,
Где делает бездарь из них колодки,
В господском смысле он, конечно, хам.

Поэт он гимны всем семи грехам,
Непревзойденный с митинговой глотке.
Историков о нем тоскуют плетки
Пройтись по всем стихозопотрохам…

В иных условиях и сам, пожалуй,
Он стал иным, детина этот жалый,
Кощунник, шут и пресненский апаш:
В нем слишком много удали и мощи,

Какой полны издревле наши рощи,
Уж слишком он весь Русский, слишком наш!

(Игорь Северянин, 1926)

Huge as his verses (doled out by the verse
and selling best among the ragged caste
and used by fools for stuffing shoes at most)
he's, in the feudal sense, a lout or worse.

He hymns all seven deadly sins in bursts
of party-meeting passion unsurpassed.
Whips in hand, historians burrow, thirsting
for him, through the entrails of his verse...

In other settings he would, very like,
be different, this big and crazy bloke,
blasphemer, beatnik, jester that he is.
There's too much boldness in him, too much power

like that which fills those ancient woods of ours,
too much of all of Russia, too much of us.

(Igor Severyanin, 1926)

ПАСТЕРНАК

Когда в поэты тщится Пастернак,
Разумничает Недоразуменье.
Мое о нем ему нелестно мненье:
Не отношусь к нему совсем никак.

Им восторгаются – плачевный знак.
Но я не прихожу в недоуменье:
Чем бестолковее стихотворенье,
Тем глубже смысл находит в нем простак.

Безглавых тщательноголовый пастырь
Усердно подновляет гниль и застарь
И бестолочь выделывает. Глядь,

Состряпанное потною бездарью
Пронзает в мозг Ивана или Марью,
За гения принявших заурядь.

(Игорь Северянин, 29.3.1928)

When he plays at poetry, Pasternak
speaks with the sly voice of misunderstanding,
and if it's my opinion you're demanding:
opinions of him I entirely lack.

They rave about him – that's the sorry fact.
But I don't rate confusion. It's outstanding:
the more his sillyness goes on expanding,
the more profound he's seen as by the pack.

This careful-minded minder of the mindless
reworks with zeal the rot long left behind us
and make's an utter pig's ear of it. See –

how stuff cooked up by this wet, clueless larry
injects the brain of each Tom, Dick or Harry
that sees a genius in nonentity.

(Igor Severyanin, 29 March 1928)

АННЕ АХМАТОВОЙ

Мне кажется, я подберу слова,
Похожие на вашу первозданность.
А ошибусь, – мне это трын-трава,
Я все равно с ошибкой не расстанусь.

Я слышу мокрых кровель говорок,
Торцовых плит заглохшие эклоги.
Какой-то город, явный с первых строк,
Растет и отдается в каждом слоге.

Кругом весна, но за город нельзя.
Еще строга заказчица скупая.
Глаза шитьем за лампою слезя,
Горит заря, спины не разгибая.

Вдыхая дали ладожскую гладь,
Спешит к воде, смиряя сил упадок.
С таких гулянок ничего не взять.
Каналы пахнут затхлостью укладок.

По ним ныряет, как пустой орех,
Горячий ветер и колышет веки
Ветвей и звезд, и фонарей, и вех,
И с моста вдаль глядящей белошвейки.

Бывает глаз по-разному остер,
По-разному бывает образ точен.
но самой страшной крепости раствор –
Ночная даль под взглядом белой ночи.

TO ANNA AKHMATOVA

It seems to me that I've found just the words
to sum up your primordial quality.
If I'm mistaken – well, so what? Who cares?
Mistakes like this I'll stick to, anyway.

I hear the roof-tops chatter in the rain,
a fading pastoral on wooden tiles.
Some town springs up – that's clear from the first lines –,
with each new syllable its form reveals.

Spring's everywhere, roads out of town are swamped.
The penny-pinching customer still frowns.
Eyes smarting from long sewing by the lamp,
the dawn won't pause to stretch, but burns and burns

till, breathing in Lagoda's smooth wide surface,
she summons strength, comes quickly to the shore.
Yet in the end such trips serve little purpose:
the canal smells like a musty chest of drawers.

Across its surface, like an empty nutshell
a hot wind bounces, blinks the eyelids of
stars, street-lamps, branches – and the seamstress, as she
stares at the distance from the bridge above.

An eye can have such different kinds of keenness,
an image can be sharp in different ways,
yet there's an fissure in the strongest fortress –
a patch of dark night under white night's gaze.

Таким я вижу облик ваш и взгляд.
Он мне внушен не тем столбом из соли,
Которым вы пять лет тому назад
Испуг оглядки к рифме прикололи,

Но, исходив от ваших первых книг,
Где крепли прозы пристальной крупицы,
Он и во всех, как искры проводник,
Событья былью заставляет биться.

(Борис Пастернак, 1928)

That's how I see your gaze and see your profile.
It's not suggested to me by that column
of salt with which, five years ago, you fixed
the fear of looking back into your rhyme,

but comes instead from those first books of yours
where vital prose was sprouting its first grain,
and it's in everything, like sparks in wires,
causing the past to pulse with life again.

(Boris Pasternak, 1928)

ПОДРАЖАНИЕ И Ф. АННЕНСКОМУ

И с тобой, моей первой причудой,
Я простился. Восток голубел.
Просто молвила: "Я не забуду".
Я не сразу поверил тебе.

Возникают, стираются лица,
Мил сегодня, а завтра далек.
Отчего же на этой странице
Я когда-то загнул уголок?

И всегда открывается книга
В том же месте. И странно тогда:
Всё как будто с прощального мига
Не прошли невозвратно года.

О, сказавший, что сердце из камня,
Знал наверно: оно из огня…
Никогда не пойму, ты близка мне
Или только любила меня.

(Анна Ахматова, 20 февраля 1911)

And so now, first caprice of mine, I let
you go. The east has turned a deeper blue.
You simply said the words: "I shan't forget".
At the time I didn't believe them to be true.

Faces appear from nowhere – are erased
again, today so dear, tomorrow flown
into the distance. Is that why at this page
some time ago I turned the corner down?

Since then the book has always fallen open
at the same place, and then, strangely, it seems
like everything that followed that one moment
of parting, all those lost years, had never been.

The heart's said to be a stone: I always knew
that it's a fire. Yet one thing's quite above me:
were you ever really someone who
was close to me – or did you only love me?

(Anna Akhmatova, 20 February 1911)

УЧИТЕЛЬ

(Памяти Иннокентия Анненского)

А тот, кого учителем считаю,
Как тень прошел и тени не оставил
Весь яд впитал, всю эту одурь выпил,
И славы ждал, и славы не дождался,
Кто был предвестьем, предзнаменованьем
Всего, что с нами после совершилось,
Всех пожалел, во всех вдохнул томленье –
И задохнулся…

(Анна Ахматова, 1945)

TEACHER
(In memory of Innokentij Annensky)

...and he whom I called teacher slid away
like a shadow, left no shadows in his wake.
He'd drained the poison dry, drunk in its stupour,
awaited glory: glory never came.
Who was a kind of portent, harbinger
of all that was to happen to us later,
who suffered with all, suffused us all with langour.
        ...who suffocated...

(Anna Akhmatova, 1945)

ПАМЯТИ АХМАТОВОЙ

1.

Ахматова двувременной была.
О ней и плакать как-то не пристало.
Не верилось, когда она жила,
не верилось, когда ее не стало.

Она ушла, как будто бы напев
уходит в глубь темнеющего сада.
Она ушла, как будто бы навек,
вернулась в Петербург из Ленинграда.

Она связала эти времена
в туманно-теневое средоточье,
И если Пушкин – солнце, то она
в поэзии пребудет белой ночью.

Над смертью и бессмертьем, вне всего,
она лежала, как бы между прочим,
не в настоящем, а поверх него
лежала между будущим и прошлым.

И прошлое у гроба тихо шло
не вереницей дам богоугодных.
Седые челки гордо и светло
мерцали из-под шляпок старомодных.

Да, изменила время их черты,
красавиц той, когдатошней России,
но их глаза – лампады доброты –
ни крутоверть, ни мгла не загасили.

Шло будущее, слабое в плечах.
Шли мальчики. Они себя сжигали
пожаром гимназическим в очах
и в кулаках тетрадочки сжимали.

1.

She spanned two ages, and it seems as if
it's out of place to mourn her death.
So unbelievable a life: who could believe
its dying breath?

She left us like a melody slowly fading
from a garden's shade,
she left, as if eternally receding
to Petersburg from Leningrad.

She gathered up the scattered times that we
inhabit in her misty light,
and if Pushkin's our poetry's bright sun, then she's
its white summer night.

She lay beyond life and death, indeed, she lay
beyond everything,
apart from the world, and incidental, free,
quietly hovering

beyond all time. The past slid by her tomb:
a slow – though not a pious – procession
of women, grey hair glinting proudly under
bonnets long out of fashion.

Though time has changed their features, and their beauty's
of a Russia long gone by,
their eyes, like kindly lanterns, never falter,
grow dim, or die.

The Future slid by, shoulders weak with youth:
schoolboys, their eyes ablaze
with learning's flame, their books gripped tight in their
clenched fingers. And girls,

И девочки в портфельчиках своих
несли, наверно, дневники и списки.
Все те же – из блаженных и святых –
наивные российские курсистки.

И ты, распад всемирный, не убий
ту связь времен, – она еще поможет.
Ведь просто быть не может двух Россий,
как быть и двух Ахматовых не может.

2.

Ну, а в другом гробу, невдалеке,
как будто рядом с библией частушка,
лежала в белом простеньком платке
ахматовского возраста старушка.

Лежала, как готовилась к венцу,
устав стирать, мести, скрести и штопать,
крестьянка по рукам и по лицу,
а в общем, домработница, должно быть.

быть мертвой – это райское житье.
За ней так добро люди приглядели
и словно перед праздником дите
и вымыли и чисто приодели.

Цветами ее, правда, не почли,
но был зато по мерке гроб подогнан,
и дали туфли новые почти,
с квиточками ремонта на подошвах.

Была она прощающе ясна
и на груди благоговейно сжала
сухие руки, будто бы она
невидимую свечку в них держала

carrying satchels. What's in them? Probably
lists, and diaries – things most precious
and almost holy to the untroubled
young schoolgirls of Russia.

As for you, disintegrating powers, leave us
at least this continuity.
For two Russias, or two Akhmatovas,
there cannot be.

2.

In an adjacent coffin there lay, like a folk tune
next to a bible, the body of a
second woman, dressed in simple white linen,
the same age as Akhmatova.

She lay there like a bride-to-be, worn out
with washing, darning, scrubbing floors
and stairs. Her face, her hands left little doubt:
a peasant woman. Death, of course,

after such a life must be paradise. The neighbours
had attended to the body
with kind hands, washed her, dressed her in clean clothes
as if for a children's party,

and though it's true she wasn't decked with flowers,
the coffin was a good fit,
and they'd given her slippers, almost new – one still bore
the cobbler's receipt.

She lay, forgivingly serene, and on her breast
she reverently clasped
her shrivelled hands, as if her fingers pressed
round an invisible candle. All tasks

Они умели в жизни все уметь
писали, правда, только закорюки,
тяжелые и темные, как медь,
ни разу не целованные руки.

И думал я: а может быть, а вдруг,
но все же существуют две России:
Россия духа и Россия рук –
две разные страны, совсем чужие?!

Никто о той старушке не скорбел.
Никто ее в бессмертные не прочил.
И был над нею отстраненно бел
Ахматовой патрицианский профиль.

Ахматова превыше всех осанн
покоилась презрительно и сухо,
осознавая свой духовный сан
над самозванством и плебейством духа.

Аристократка! Вся оттуда, где
под рысаками билась мостовая!
Но руки на цветах, как на воде,
покачивались, что-то выдавая.

Они творили, как могли, добро,
но силы временами было мало,
и, легкое для Пушкина, перо
с усмешкой пальцы женские ломало.

Забыли пальцы холодок Аи,
и поцелуи в Ницце, Петербурге,
и, на груди сведенные, они
крестьянскою усталостю набухли.

those hands were given they'd accomplished capably,
though she could barely scrawl
her name: those hands, heavy and dark as copper,
that had never been kissed. And all

at once I thought: yes – two Russias! Here, intertwined,
are two quite separate lands!
– a Russia of the spirit, of the mind,
and a Russia of the hands!

No one mourned the death of that old woman,
or prayed for her soul, but above her,
there hovered, white, ever-present, the patrician
profile of Akhmatova.

Yes, Akhmatova, beyond all praise, disdainful,
aloof, and knowing her high rôle
over the commonness and the impostures
of the human soul.

An aristocrat! Yes, from where the wide streets rumble
with hooves all day!
Yet her hands, in a sea of flowers, seemed to tremble,
as if giving some secret away.

They'd worked with all their strength, though that strength failed
at times, and then the pen –
so light a tool in Pushkin's hands – rebelled,
and snapped her fingers with a grin.

Those hands forgot the kisses and the chill
of wine in Petersburg and Nice
and lay now clasped upon her bosom, filled
with peasant tiredness.

Царица без короны и жезла,
среди даров почтительности тусклых,
была она прощающе ясна,
как та старушка в тех дареных туфлях.

Ну, а старушка в том, другом гробу
лежала, не увидевшая Ниццы,
с ахматовским величием на лбу,
и между ними не было границы.

(Евгени Евтушенко, 1966)

Among the gifts of dim deference, a queen
without crown or sceptre,
like that old woman – forgivingly serene –
with her donated slippers.

And the old woman? She lay in the other coffin, and though
she'd never seen Nice, it's true,
Akhmatovan grandeur lay on her brow,
and nothing divided the two.

(Yevgeny Yevtushenko, 1966)

МАЯКОВСКИЙ В 1913 ГОДУ

Я тебя в твоей не знала славе,
Помню только бурный твой рассвет,
Но, быть может, я сегодня вправе
Вспомнить день тех отдаленных лет.
Как в стихах твоих крепчали звуки,
Новые роились голоса…
Не ленились молодые руки,
Грозные ты возводил леса.
Все, чего касался ты, казалось
Не таким, как было до тех пор,
То, что разрушал ты, – разрушалось,
В каждом слове бился приговор.
Одинок и часто недоволен,
С нетерпеньем торопил судьбу,
Знал, что скоро выйдешь весел, волен
На свою великую борьбу.
И уже отзывный гул прилива
Слышался, когда ты нам читал,
Дождь косил свои глаза гневливо,
С городом ты в буйный спор вступал.
И еще не слышанное имя
Молнией влетело в душный зал,
Чтобы ныне, всей страной хранимо,
Зазвучать, как боевой сигнал.

(Анна Ахматова 1940)

Although I didn't know your days of glory
I was present at your tempestuous dawn
and today I'll take a small step back in history
to remember, as I'm entitled to, times gone.
With every line, your words increased in power!
Unheard-of voices gathering in swarms!
Those were no idle hands that threw up such towering
and menacing new forms!
Everything you touched suddenly seemed
somehow altered, different than before,
and whatever you destroyed, remained
that way, and in every syllable the roar
of judgement. Often dissatisfied, alone,
driven on by an impatient fate,
you knew how fast the time was nearing when
you'd leap, excited, joyful, to the fight.
We could hear, as we listened to you read,
the reverberating thunder of the waters
and the downpour squinted angrily as you slid
into your wild confrontations with the city.
Your name, in those days unfamiliar, flashed
like streaks of lightning through the stuffy hall.
It's with us still today, remembered, cherished
throughout the land, a thundering battle call.

(Anna Akhmatova, 1940)

Вы ушли,
       как говорится,
               в мир в иной.
Пустота…
       Летите,
           в звезды врезываясь.
Ни тебе аванса,
          ни пивной.
Трезвость.
Нет, Есенин,
       это
          не насмешка.
В горле
     горе комом –
          не смешок.
Вижу –
     взрезанной рукой помешкав,
собственных
         костей
             качаете мешок.
Прекратите!
        Бросьте!
            Вы в своем уме ли?
Дать,
    чтоб щеки
        заливал
             смертельный мел?!
Вы ж
    такое
        загибать умели,
Что другой
       на свете
           не умел.
Почему?
      Зачем?
           Недоуменье смяло.
Критики бормочут:

You've left us,
                as they say,
                            and gone off cruising
through emptiness,
                to other worlds
                            beyond the stars.
There's no more credit for you,
                            no more boozing,
no more bars.
No, Yesenin,
            I'm
                not trying to take the piss
this lump in my throat's
                    not laughter,
                            but bitter moans.
I see you, hand slashed open,
                        round the twist,
swing back and forth,
                a sack
                    of your own bones.
Stop!
    Pack it in!
                Have you gone mad or what?
Letting
    your cheeks
                go white like that,
                            like death!?
For turning things
                around
                    you'd always got
the knack,
        and better
                than anyone else on earth.
Why?
    What was gained?
                    Astonishment confuses.
The critics mumbled:

75

— этому вина

то…

  да се…

    а главное,

      что смычки мало,

в результате

    много пива и вина. —

Дескать,

   заменить бы вам

      богему

        классом,

класс влиял на вас,

     и было б не до драк.

Ну, а класс-то

    жажду

      заливает квасом?

Класс — он тоже

    выпить

      не дурак.

Дескать,

   к вам приставить бы

      кого из напостов —

стали б

   содержанием

      премного одаренней.

Вы бы

  в день

    писали

      строк по сто,

утомительно

   и длинно

      как Доронин.

А по-моему,

   осуществись

      такая бредь,

на себя бы

   раньше наложили руки.

"his failure's due, we think
to this…
            or that…
                        but the main trouble is,
                                    he loses
the thread, because of too much
                        of the drink…"
They say
            if you'd swapped
                        decadence
                                    for Class
you'd have been changed,
                        and avoided heavy scenes.
You think
            the working-class
                        gets off on kvass?
In drinking matters
                        they're not
                                    exactly green.
They say
            if there'd been
                        someone to keep you under
control,
            your talent
                        might have started soaring.
But
      you'd have written,
                        day after day,
                                    hundreds
of lines
            as long as Doronin's
                        and just as boring.
I know
            if I'd produced
                        that kind of crap
I'd also
            be bent on self-eradication.

Лучше уж
            от водки умереть,
чем от скуки!
Не откроют
            нам
                        причин потери
ни плетля,
            ни ножик перочинный.
Может,
        окажись
                    чернила в "Англетере",
Вены
    резать
            не было б причины.
Подражатели обрадовались:
                                    бис!
Над собою
            чуть не взвод
                        расправу учинил.
Почему же
            увеличивать
                        число самоубийств?
Лучше
    увеличь
            изготовление чернил!
Навсегда
        теперь
                язык
                    в зубах затворится.
Тяжело
        и неуместно
                    разводить мистерии.
У народа,
        у языкотворца,
умер
    звонкий
            забулдыга подмастерье.

But I'd far rather
                    vodka wipe me off the map
than bored frustration.
The reason
            for so much blood
                                pointlessly spilled
neither noose
            nor pocket-knife explains.
If
   the Angleterre's inkwells
                            only had been filled
there mightn't
                have been a need
                                for slashing veins.
Imitators cheered:
                    Encore! Encore!
Whole platoons
                were poised for
                                self-destruction.
We've suicides
            enough –
                    why raise the score?
Better
        to raise
            the rate of ink production.
The tongue's
            now locked
                        behind the teeth
                                        for good.
Such mystery-making's
                        serious,
                                and absurd.
The nation,
            and the wordsmiths' brotherhood
have lost
        the apprentice-drunkard
                                of the word.

И несут
        стихов заупокойный лом,
с прошлых
         с похорон
               не переделавши почти.
В холм
       тупые рифми
             загонять колом –
разве так
       поэта
           надо бы почтить?
Вам
     и памятник еще не слит, –
где он,
       бронзы звон
            или гранита грань? –
а к решеткам памяти
               уже
                  понанесли
посвящений
         и воспоминаний дрань.
Ваше имя
        в платочки рассоплено,
ваше слово
         слюнявит Собинов
и выводит
         под березкой дохлой –
"Ни слова,
       о дру-уг мой,
              ни вздо-о-о-о-ха".
Эх,
    поговорить бы иначе
с этим самым
              с Леонидом Лоэнгринычем!
Встать бы здесь
           гремящим скандалистом:
Не позволю

The people come
                with their supply of trashy verse,
unchanged
            from previous deaths,
                            regurgitated,
defile your grave
                with doggerel
                            or worse –
Is that
        how poet's lives
                        are celebrated?
Your monument
                still hasn't been erected.
Where is it –
                the ringing bronze,
                                the granite hunk?
The railing's there, though:
                            and on it
                                    they've inflicted
a load
        of verbose and nostalgic junk.
I hear your name
                in little hankies snivelled.
Sobinov quotes you,
                    drools your verse to death.
Beneath the withered birch
                        you hear him drivel:
"Not a wor-r-r-d,
                my f-r-r-riend,
                            no-o-o, not a b-r-r-reath…"
Oh,
    I really can't find an expletive which is
strong enough for these
                        Lohengriniches!
I ought to drum up
                a thundering great scandal.
I can't see

мямлить стих
и мять! –
Оглушить бы
их
трехпалым свистом
в бабушку
и в бога душу мать!
Чтобы
разнеслась
бездарнейшая погань,
раздувая
темь
пиджачных парусов,
чтобы врассыпную
разбежался Коган,
встреченных
увеча
пиками усов.
Дрянь
пока что
мало поредела.
Дела много –
только поспевать.
Надо
жизнь
сначала переделать,
переделав –
можно воспевать.
Это время –
трудновато для пера,
но скажите,
вы,
калеки и калекши,
где,
когда,
какой великий выбирал
путь,

                poetry
                            mutilated – tell
them where to go, yes
                            whistle out
                                        these vandals,
tell them to bugger off and go to hell!

Let's
        rid ourselves
                        of talentless infections,
blast coat-tails
                till
                        they billow like black sails,
see Kogan
                scattered out in all directions –
and who cares
                who
                        his spiked moustache impales!
There's still
                a lot of crap
                            around these days
and much to do
                just to keep up with things.
Human life
                must learn
                            to change its ways.
Once it's changed,
                then its praises can be sung.
It's true, these times
                are hard ones for the pen
but tell me,
            you
                wimps and cripples of today:
where
        is there a single one
                            of all great men
who chose

чтобы протоптанней
                    и легше?
Слово –
        полководец
                    человечьей силы.
Марш!
      Чтоб время
                сзади
                      ядрами рвалось.
К старым дням
              чтоб ветром
                          относило
только
       путаницу волос.
Для веселия
            планета наша
                          мало оборудована.
Надо
     вырвать
             радость
                     у грядущих дней.
В этой жизнь
             помереть
                       не трудно.
Сделать жизнь
              значительно трудней.

(Владимир Маяковски, 1926)

                the trodden path,
                            the easier way?
The word's
            the captain of all man's powers.
                                        March on!
Let time
        break through
                        with bullets
                                    from behind!
Leave nothing
            to the old days
                            past and gone
except for
            the hair that's ruffled by the wind.
We're ill-equipped
                to build
                            a happy world.
So
    tear joy
            from the days
                            as they arrive!
In this life
            to die's
                    not difficult.
It's hard as hell
                to be alive.

(Vladimir Mayakovsky, 1926)

85

ЕСЕНИН

Он в жизнь вбегал рязанским простаком,
Голубоглазым, кудреватым, русым,
С задорным носом и веселым вкусом,
К усладам жизни солнышком влеком.

Но вскоре бунт швырнул свой грязный ком
В сиянье глаз. Отравленный укусом
Змей мятежа, злословил над Иисусом,
Сдружиться постарался с кабаком…

В кругу разбойников и проституток,
Томясь от богохульных прибауток,
Он понял, что кабак ему поган…

И Богу вновь раскрыл, раскаясь, сени
Неистовой души своей Есенин,
Благочестивый русский хулиган…

(Игорь Северянин, 1925)

YESENIN

A simpleton from Ryazan, he came diving
into life, with curly locks, blue eyes,
a cocky turned-up nose and happy ways,
and sunny liking for the joys of living.

But soon rebellion threw its dirty slubs
in his blue eyes, set loose the toxic dragon
of mutiny. He blasphemed Jesus, took an
unhealthy interest in the seedier pubs.

He hung out with the thieves and whores a while
till, plagued by godless rhymes, he saw how vile
these places were – he wouldn't be a fool again.

And thus to God re-opens (thunder-roll)
the vestibule of the chaotic soul
of Yesenin, the pious Russian hooligan.

(Igor Severyanin, 1925)

МЕТЕЛЬ

Февраль – любовь и гнев погоды.
И, странно воссияв окрест,
великим севером природы
очнулась скудость дачных мест.

И улица в четыре дома,
открыв длину и ширину,
берёт себе непринуждённо
весь снег вселенной, всю луну.

Как сильно вьюжит! Не иначе –
метель посвящена тому,
кто эти дерева и дачи
так близко принимал к уму.

Ручья невзрачное теченье
сосну, понурившую ствол,
в иное он вовлёк значенье
и в драгоценность произвёл.

Не потому ль, в красе и тайне,
пространство, загрустив о нём,
той речи бред и бормотанье
имеет в голосе своём.

И в снегопаде, долго бывшем,
вдруг, на мгновенье, прервалась
меж домом тем и тем кладбищем
печали пристальная связь.

(Белла Ахмадулина, 1968)

BLIZZARD
[on Boris Pasternak]

February. Love, and the weather's raging.
Across the strangely radiant land
rural poverty's awakened
by nature's giant Northern hand.

The roadway with its four houses
has opened wide its length and breadth
and casually gathers in all the snow
in the universe, and the whole moon with it.

How thickly it's falling! No different from
those snows made holy by one who bound
these woods, this simple country home
so intimately into his mind.

The little stream on its humdrum course,
the pine-trees with their nodding crowns
– he gave them quite a different sense,
made them shine like precious stones.

Surely that's the reason why,
since mourning him, the empty space
bears the murmurs and mutterings of his tongue
in its secret, beautiful voice.

And suddenly, in a blizzard like this
that seemed to go on and on for ever,
between that graveyard and the house
an intimate, tragic bond was severed.

(Bella Akhmadulina, 1968)

ПАМЯТИ МАРИНЫ ЦВЕТАЕВОЙ

Хмуро тянется день непогожий.
Безутешно струятся ручьи
По крыльцу перед дверью прихожей
И в открытые окна мои.

За оградою вдоль по дороге
Затопляет общественный сад.
Развалившись, как звери в берлоге,
Облака в беспорядке лежат.

Мне в ненастье мерещится книга
О земле и ее красоте.
Я рисую лесную шишигу
Для тебя на заглавном листе.

Ах, Марина, давно уже время,
Да и труд не такой уж ахти,
Твой заброшенный прах в реквиеме
Из Елабуги перенести.

Торжество твоего переноса
Я задумывал в прошлом году
Над снегами пустынного плеса,
Где зимуют баркасы во льду.

(Борис Пастернак)

Gloomily the rainy day drags by.
Inconsolable, the water drains
in streams onto the porch that shelters my
front door, drips in through open windows-panes.

All along the track beyond the fence
allotments are completely under water.
Like wild animals sprawled in their dens
the clouds lie scattered in complete disorder.

This stormy weather seems to me like some
great book about the earth and all its glory.
I'll draw for you a little forest-gnome
on the first page by the title of the story.

Oh, Marina, so much time has passed,
besides, it's not a painful task to bring
your long neglected ashes back at last
from Yelabuga in this requiem.

With all due ceremony I prepared,
a year ago now, for this enterprise
across the miles of snowed-up river-beds
where barges winter, locked up in the ice.

(Boris Pasternak)

ПАМЯТИ СЕРГЕЯ ЕСЕНИНА

…И не жалость – мало жил,
И не горечь – мало дал, –
Много жил – кто в *наши* жил
Дни, *всё* дал – кто песню дал.

(Марина Цветаева, 1926)

IN MEMORY OF SERGEI YESENIN

I feel no regret that he lived but little,
Nor bitterness that he gave but little –
For to live in our times was to live to the full,
And he who gave us his song – gave all.

(Marina Tsvetaeva, 1926)

"...Дорога не скажу куда...".
(Анна Ахматова)

Пластинки глупенькое чудо,
проигрыватель – вздор какой,
и слышно, как невесть откуда,
из недр стеснённых, из-под спуда
корней, сопревших трав и хвой,
где закипает перегной,
вздымая пар до небосвода,
нет, глубже мыслимых глубин,
из пекла, где пекут рубин
и начинается природа, –
исторгнут, близится, и вот
донёсся бас земли и вод,
которым молвлено протяжно,
как будто вовсе без труда,
так легкомысленно, так важно:
"...Дорога не скажу куда..."

Меж нами так не говорят,
нет у людей такого знанья,
не вымыслом, ни наугад
тому не подыскать названья,
что мы, в невежестве своём,
строкой бессмертной назовем.

(Белла Ахмадулина, 1968)

A LINE

"...where the road leads I shall not say..."
(Anna Akhmatova)

The vinyl disc's a silly wonder,
the stereo a trivial toy:
just hear how it, from some obscure and
cramped interior, buried under
roots, grass clippings, where the soil
builds up its heat and starts to boil,
its vapour rising on the winds,
no, deeper – from the depths of hell,
where rubies bake, and where the whole
of nature has its origins –
how it ejects and sets in motion
the great bass voice of earth and ocean...
But then, the murmured overlay,
soft, without the slightest straining,
so casual, yet filled with meaning:
"...where the road leads I shall not say..."

Worlds different from the way we chatter.
No one, by chance or fantasy,
nor those with knowledge of such matters
could put a name to that which we
in our sweet ignorance define
simply as "that immortal line".

(Bella Akhmadulina, 1968)

95

[Н. Гумилеву]

В ремешках пенал и книги были,
Возвращалась я домой из школы.
Эти липы, верно, не забыли
Нашей встречи, мальчик мой веселый.
Только, ставши лебедем надменным,
Изменился серый лебеденок.
А на жизнь мою лучом нетленным
Грусть легла, и голос мой незвонок.

(Анна Ахматова, 1912)

Он любил три вещи на свете:
За вечерней пенье, белых павлинов
И стертые карты Америки,
Не любил, когда плачут дети,
Не любил чая с малиной
И женской истерики.
…А я была его женой.

(Анна Ахматова, 1911)

[to Gumilev]

My satchel filled with pencil box and books,
I used to take this way back home from school.
These linden trees, surely, cannot have forgotten
our encounters here, carefree boy of mine.
But the arrogant swan has been transformed into
a small grey cygnet. Over my life has fallen,
indestructible, a ray of sorrow,
and my voice has no sound.

(Anna Akhmatova, 1912)

Three things he loved in this world:
white peacocks, a twilight melody
and tattered maps of America.
But he hated it when the kids yelled
and he hated jam with his tea
and he hated female hysterics
– and yet he was married... to me!

(Anna Akhmatova, 1911)

ПАМЯТИ АННЕНСКОГО

К таким нежданным и певучим бредням
    Зовя с собой умы людей,
Был Иннокентий Анненский последним
    Из царскосельских лебедей.

Я помню дни: я, робкий, торопливый,
    Входил в высокий кабинет,
Где ждал меня спокойный и учтивый,
    Слегка седеющий поэт.

Десяток фраз, пленительных и странных,
    Как бы случайно уроня,
Он вбрасывал в пространство безымянных
    Мечтаний – слабого меня.

О сумрак отступающие вещи
    И еле слышные духи,
И этот голос, нежный и зловещий,
    Уже читающий стихи!

В них плакала какая-то обида,
    Звенела медь и шла гроза,
А там, над шкафом, профиль Эврипида
    Слепил горящие глаза.

…Скамью я знаю в парке; мне сказали,
    Что он любил сидеть на ней,
Замдучиво смотря, как сини дали
    В червонном золоте аллей.

Там вечером и страшно и красиво,
    В тумане светит мрамор плит,
И женщина, как серна боязлива,
    Во тьме к прохожему спешит.

IN MEMORY OF INNOKENTIY ANNENSKY

He drew with startling and melodious arts
     the souls and minds of all his fellow-
countrymen: Annensky was the last
     of all the swans of Tsarsky Selo.

That day when, shy, impatiently, I entered
     the poet's spacious study, where
he waited for me, courteous, calm and centred,
     with his slightly greying hair…

A dozen phrases, captivating, strange,
     let fall as if by purest chance,
left me weak, defenceless, seemed to plunge
     me into a space of nameless dreams.

All things began to merge into the dusk:
     a faintest perfume in the air –
then in that voice, so gentle, ominous,
     his poetry, so familiar!

The clang of copper, and the thunder's blast,
     the sobbing, too, of deep malaise!
From its place on the cabinet the bust
     of Euripides flashes ardent eyes.

In the park's a bench where, I've been told,
     he often liked to sit and rest,
gazing down the avenue's pure gold
     into deep blue distances.

In the evening mist a marble headstone,
     beautiful yet fearsome, gleams,
and a young woman, timid as a fawn
     hurries past him through the gloom.

Она глядит, она поет и плачет,
И снова плачет и поет,
Не понимая, что всё это значит,
Но только чувствуя – не тот.

Журчит вода, протачивая шлюзы,
Сырой травою пахнет мгла,
И жалок голос одинокой музы,
Последней – Царского Села.

(Николай Гумилев, 1911)

She looks about her, sings, and weeps, and then
  repeats her sobbing and her song.
She doesn't understand what all this means
  but only feels: *this* must be wrong.

The water as it passes through the sluices
  is murmuring. The darkness smells of
damp grass. And the sad voice of a muse is
  heard – last, lonely muse of Tsarsky Selo.

(Nikolai Gumilev, 1911)

101

ГУМИЛЕВ

Путь конквистадора в горах остер.
Цветы романтики над ним нависли.
И жемчуга на дне – морские мысли –
Трехцветились, когда ветрел костер.

И путешественник, войдя в шатер,
В стихах свои писания описьмил.
Уж как Европа Африку не высмей,
Столп огненный – души ее простор.

Кто из поэтов спел бы живописней
Того, кто в жизнь одну десятки жизней
Умел вместить? Любовник, зверобой,

Солдат – все было в рыцарской манере…
Он о земле тоскует на Венере,
Вооружась подзорную трубой.

(Игорь Северянин, 1926-1927)

The mountain path of the conquistador
was harsh. Romantic flowers drooped over him.
And sea thoughts – pearls by day – at nightfall gleamed
tri-coloured when the breeze blew through the fire.

And once inside his tent, the traveller
composed his letters, manuscripts in rhyme.
For Africa's not carved in Europe's form,
the vastness of her soul's a flaming pillar.

What poet could sing vividly of one
who seemed to live within one lifetime ten
or more, who as a lover, as hunter, and

as soldier showed the marks of knightly birth?
Now he looks down longingly on earth
from Venus, with a telescope in hand.

(Igor Severyanin, 1926-1927)

ПАМЯТИ СЕРГЕЯ ЕСЕНИНА

Так просто можно жизнь покинуть эту,
Бездумно и безбольно догореть.
Но не дано Российскому поэту
Такою светлой смертью умереть.

Всего верней свинец душе крылатой
Небесные откроет рубежи,
Иль хриплый ужас лапою косматой
Из сердца, как из губки, выжмет жизнь.

(Анна Ахматова, 1925)

IN MEMORY OF SERGEI YESENIN

It's so simple to leave this life behind,
burn away, thoughtless, painless, in a last breath,
but a Russian poet isn't destined
to die such an easy death.

Most likely for the true, winged soul
a bullet will open heaven's range,
or hoarse terror with its shaggy paw
wring life from the heart, as from a sponge.

(Anna Akhmatova, 1925)

[Б. Ахмадулиной]

Какое равенство? Смугла и пышнокрыла,
Вся в черном бархате, как южной ночи мгла,
Явилась яркая, всех бабочек затмила,
Витражных, пламенных смежила два крыла,
Зубчато-сводчата и недемократична,
Перепорхнула вдруг и села на рукав,
Так в скобках в адресе указывают: "Лично",
К тому из спорящих, кто, мнилось, был не прав.

К тому из спорящих, кто жизнь в нелучшем виде
Нам предлагал любить, увы, какая есть:
И в смерти равенства нет тоже, не взыщите.
Нерона помнят все, а те, чья кровь и честь
Им были втоптаны в грязь римскую, – забыты.
Мигала бабочка, прижавшись к рукаву,
Несправедливости подружка и Обиды.
А где, скажи, еще ей приклонить главу?

(Александр Кушнер)

[To Bella Akhmadulina]

What's that about equality? Tanned, superb,
in velvet, black as Mediterranean night,
she entered, radiant, eclipsing the butterflies,
folded stained-glass wings aflame and bright,
serrated-edged and scarcely democratic –
then fluttered round, to land, as if she were
an envelope marked "personal" in brackets,
on the arm of one she'd argued with before,

the one who'd said that we should love reality,
not as ideal, but as, alas, it is,
that death brings no atonement, no equality –
We all know Nero, but who knows of those
whose blood and pride he crushed in Roman mud...
The butterfly flutters, then grips his arm instead
– she, friend of the unjustly suffering crowd...
But where else, tell me, could she lay her head?

(Alexander Kushner)

БЛОК

Красив, как Демон Врубеля для женщин,
Он лебедем казался, чье перо
Белей, чем облако и серебро,
Чей стан дружил, как то ни странно, с френчем.

Благожелательный к меньшим и меньшим,
Дерзал – поэтно – видеть в зле добро.
Взлетал. Срывался. В дебрях мысли брел.
Любил Любовь и Смерть, двумя увенчан.

Он тщетно на земле любви искал:
Ее здесь нет. Когда же свой оскал
Явила Смерть, он понял: – Незнакомка…

У рая слышен легкий хруст шагов:
Подходит Блок. С ним – от его стихов
Лучащаяся – странничья котомка…

(Игорь Северянин, 1925)

As handsome to the women as Vrubel's
"Demon", he was like a swan, whose down
is white as snow or silver, and yet on
the other hand, a uniform stood him well.

Well-wishing to the least, the weak, he dared,
poetically, to see the good in evil
– took off, broke free, then roamed a mental jungle
in love with Love and Death, the royal pair.

He searched the earth for love – in vain, for none
is to be found. And when he saw Death's grin
he knew it was the Unknown Woman waiting.

In heaven they hear the crunch of footsteps: Blok
is coming with his wanderer's shoulder-pack,
from which verse after verse is radiating.

(Igor Severyanin, 1925)

КОГДА Я ДУМАЮ О БЛОКЕ...

Когда я думаю о Блоке,
когда тоскую по нему,
то вспоминаю я не строки,
а мост, пролетку и Неву.
И над ночными голосами
чеканный облик седока –
круги под страшными глазами
и черный очерк сюртука.
Летят навстречу светы, тени
дробятся звезды в мостовых,
и что-то выше, чем смятенье,
в сплетенье пальцев восковых.
И, как в загадочном прологе,
чья суть смутна и глубока,
в тумане тают стук пролетки,
булыжник, Блок, облака...

(Евгений Евтушенко)

Whenever Blok comes to my mind,
when I yearn for him, I never
think of some line that he penned,
but a bridge, a coach, the river.
In the web of night-time voices
there's a rider's figure set,
with a sunken eye that flashes,
frock-coat's inky silhouette.
Lights and shadows fly to meet him,
stars fall, shatter on the street,
wax-white fingers hint at more than
worry in the way they meet.
Then, as if in some strange prologue
that's profound and yet unclear
mist enshrouds the rumbling carriage:
clouds, Blok, cobbles – disappear...

(Yevgeny Yevtushenko)

111

АХМАТОВА

Послушница обители Любви
Молитвенно перебирает четки.
Осенней ясностью в ней чувства четки.
Удел – до святости непоправим.

Он, Найденный, как сердцем ни зови,
Не будет с ней в своей гордыне кроткий
И гордый в кротости, уплывший в лодке
Рекой из собственной ее крови…

Уж вечер. Белая взлетает стая.
У белых стен скорбит она, простая.
Кровь капает, как розы, изо рта.

Уже осталось крови в ней немного,
Но ей не жаль ее во имя бога;
Ведь розы крови – розы для креста…

(Игорь Северянин, 1925)

Obedient novice of Love's holy dwelling,
She reverently recites her rosary,
Sensing with an autumn clarity
Her fate before her, sacred and compelling.

The one she found, the one her heart is calling,
Won't stay with her. With proud humility,
Or gentle pride, he'll sail his boat away
Along her lifeblood's river. Evening's falling,

White flocks are taking wing. By whitewashed walls
She stands and lets the simple tears fall,
While, like red roses, little drops of blood

Run from her lips. She weakens with their loss.
Yet she does not feel sorry for her god,
For roses of blood are roses for the cross.

(Igor Severyanin, 1925)

ЦВЕТАЕВА

Блондинка с папироскою, в зеленом,
Беспочвенных безбожников божок,
Гремит в стихах про волжский бережок,
О в персянку Разине влюбленном.

Пред слушателем, мощью изумленным,
То барабана дробный говорок,
то друга дева, свой свершая срок,
Сопернице вручает умиленной.

То вдруг поэт, храня серьезный вид,
Таким задорным вздором удивит,
Что в даме – жар и страха дрожь – во франте…

Какие там "свершенье" ни верши,
Мертвы стоячие часы души,
Не числящиеся в ее таланте…

(Игорь Северянин, 1926)

TSVETAEVA

This blonde with cigarette and clad in green,
the idol of the idle unbelievers,
yells out her verse about the Volga river
and the Persian beauty worshipped by Razin.

Before an audience staggered by her spleen
she's first a rattling drum, then plays the diva,
handing her outdated lover over
to the next astonished rival on the scene.

Then suddenly, still with a straight expression,
she amazes with the kind of crazy passion
that makes women sweat and tremble – and makes a bloke...

But what was promising to climax – doesn't.
The timepiece of the soul droops lifeless, hasn't
the will to fire her talent with its stroke.

(Igor Severyanin, 1926)

115

МАРИНЕ ЦВЕТАЕВОЙ

Все наяву связалось – воздух самый
Вокруг тебя до самых звезд твоих,
И поясок, и каждый твой упрямый
Упругий шаг, и угловатый стих.

Ты, не отпущенная на поруки,
Вольна гореть и расточать вольна,
Подумай только: не было разлуки,
Смыкаются, как воды, времена.

На радость – руку, на печаль, на годы!
Смеженных крыл не размыкай опять:
Тебе подвластны гибельные воды,
Не надо снова их разъединять.

(Арсений Тарковский, 1941)

MARINA TSVETAEVA

All was made as one: the air itself
around you, right up to the very stars,
the belt you wear, each of your purposeful
and springy footsteps, and your jagged verse.

Since you've not been granted bail, you're free
to burn, and free to dissipate and squander.
Just think of this: it surely couldn't be
called parting, when times coalesced, like waters.

For joy, for sorrow, for the years – a hand!
Don't open up your folded wings just when
the waters of the oceans all depend
on you. Don't separate them out again.

(Arseny Tarkovsky, 1941)

ПАМЯТИ А. А. АХМАТОВА

Стелил я снежную постель,
Луга и рощи обезглавил,
К твоим ногам прильнуть заставил
Сладчайший лавр, горчайший хмель.

Но марта не сменил апрель
На страже росписей и правил.
Я памятник тебе поставил
На самой слезной из земель.

Под небом северным стою
Пред белой, бледной, непокорной
Твоею высотою горной

И сам себя не узнаю,
Один, один в рубахе черной
В твоем грядущем, как в раю.

(Арсений Тарковский, 1968)

IN MEMORY OF A. A. AKHMATOVA

I spread and smoothed the snowy sheet,
decapitated grove and glade,
took bitter hops, sweet laurel, made
them nestle down beside your feet.

But April didn't take the seat
of March to watch for truth, to guard
inventories. I've set you out
a marker in a world replete

with tears. Beneath the northern skies
I stand before your bleak and white
uncompromising mountain height

in a black shirt, to my own eyes
a stranger, lost, alone inside
your future, as in paradise.

(Arseny Tarkovsky, 1968)

119

УРОКИ МУЗЫКИ

Люблю, Марина, что тебя, как всех,
что, как меня, –
озябшею гортанью
не говорю: тебя – как свет! как снег! –
усильем шеи, будто лед глотаю,

стараюсь вымолвить: тебя, как всех,
учили музыке. (О, крах ученья!
Как если бы, под Богов плач и смех,
свече внушали правила свеченья.)

Не ладили две равных темноты:
рояль и ты – два совершенных круга,
в тоске взаимной глухонемоты
терпя иноязычие друг друга.

Два мрачных исподлобья сведены
в неразрешимой и враждебной встрече:
рояль и ты – две сильных тишины,
два слабых горла музыки и речи,

Но твоего сиротства перевес
решает дело. Что рояль? Он узник
безгласности, покуда в до-диез
мизинец свой не окунет союзник.

А ты – одна. Тебе – подмоги нет.
И музыке трудна твоя наука –
не утруждая ранящий предмет,
открыть в себе кровотеченье звука.

Марина, до! До – детства, до – судьбы,
до – ре, до – речи, до – всего, что после,
равно, как вместе мы склоняли лбы
в той общедетской предрояльной позе,

MUSIC LESSONS

I love the fact that you, like me, like so
many of us, Marina –
               (I can't speak –
my throat is frozen!) – you, like light! like snow! –
(I try to say it but I almost choke,

as if I'd swallowed ice!) – that you, you too
had piano lessons. A parody of learning!
The gods above both laugh and weep – as though
a candle could be taught the art of burning!

You and the piano, two equal darknesses,
just didn't get on: two perfect, separate rings,
miserable in the mutual deaf-muteness
of mutually exclusive foreign tongues.

Two sombre and suspicious specialists –
a hostile and impossible encounter.
you and the piano – two potent silences,
throats still too weak for speaking or resounding.

Yet your degree of orphanhood was greater
and settled the matter. Piano? – a mere prisoner
of silence, until some collaborator
presses the C sharp with her little finger.

You stood alone – no need of such liaison,
and music's struggle was, for you, to find
a way, without disturbing pain's foundations,
to open up a bleeding wound of sound.

Doh for a-*do*-lescence! Doh, Marina,
for declamation, destiny, all those
new dawning days! Alike, we bow heads in the
child-piano-player's archetypal pose –

121

как ты, как ты, вцепившись в табурет, —
о, карусель и Гедике ненужность! —
раскручивать сорвавшую берет,
свистящую вкруг головы окружность!

Марина, это всё – для красоты
придумано, в расчете на удачу
раз накричаться: я – как ты. как ты!
И с радостью бы крикнула, да – плачу.

(Белла Ахмадулина, 1963)

122

like you! like you! – to seize the piano-stool,
useless Gedike's carousel, and instead
to send the snatched-off beret into a whirl
so that it whistles round and round your head!

That's all, for good luck's sake, I meant to do:
to let for once the lovely words come leaping
out – *Marina, I'm like you, like you!*...
I meant to shout with joy, but see – I'm weeping.

(Bella Akhmadulina, 1963)

НА СМЕРТЬ БЛОКА

За туманами плыли туманы,
за луной расцветала луна…
Воспевал он лазурные страны,
где поет неземная весна.

И в туманах Прекрасная Дама
проплывала, звала вдалеке, –
словно звон отдаленного храма,
словно лунная зыбь на реке.

Узнавал он ее в трепетанье
розоватых вечерних теней
и в метелях, смятенье, молчанье
чародейной отчизны своей

Он любил ее гордо и нежно,
к ней тянулся он, строен и строг, –
но ладони ее белоснежной
бледный рыцарь коснуться не мог.

Слишком сумрачна, слишком коварна
одичалая стала земля,
и, склонившись на щит лучезарный,
оглянул он пустые поля.

И обманут мечтой несказанной,
и холодною мглой окружен,
он растаял, как месяц туманный,
как далекий молитвенный звон…

(Владимир Набоков)

Beyond the mist other mists drifted,
beyond the moon shone a strange moon.
He sang praises of blue-heavened vistas
where an unearthly spring played its tune.

In the depths of the mist the Fair Woman
drifted by, softly calling him over,
like the sound of a distant bell chiming,
like moonlight that plays on the river.

He caught sight of her form in the flutter
of shadows at closing of day,
in the snowstorms, and silence, and stutters
that over his charmed country lay.

He loved her both proudly and gently,
strove after her, stern, disciplined,
but the pallid knight never was able
to reach for her snow-white hand.

The earth grew perfidious and gloomy
the earth grew too cruel, and too wild,
and he saw only desolate meadows
as he peered out above his bright shield.

And deceived by his dreams' broken promise,
wrapped around by the chilly night air
he dissolved, like the moon into mist,
like the dying away of a prayer.

(Vladimir Nabokov)

НЕЖНОСТЬ

Разве же можно, чтоб все это
                                длилось?
Это какая-то несправедливость.
Где и когда это сделалось модным:
"Живым – равнодушье,
                                внимание – мертвым"?!
Люди сутулятся,
                выпивают.
Люди один за другим выбывают,
и произносятся для истории
нежные речи о них
                в крематории…
Что Маяковского жизни лишило?
Что револьвер ему в руку вложило?
Ему бы,
        при всем его голосе,
                                внешности,
дать бы при жизни
                хоть чуточку нежности…
Люди живые –
                они утруждают.
Нежностью только за смерть
                        награждают.

(Евгений Евтушенко, 1955)

TENDERNESS

Is this kind of thing really
                    still going on?
It doesn't seem fair, not to anyone.
When and wherever did this become fashion:
"To the living – indifference,
                    the dead – compassion"?!
The stooping comes first, then
                    the drinking starts:
One after the other, each person departs,
and for the benefit of the historians
tender speeches are made
                    in the crematoriums...
What put Mayakovsky's life to an end?
What put the revolver into his hand?
With that voice
              and those looks –
                    if he'd only been given
a small touch of tenderness while
                    he was living...
But a man when he's living's a
                  pain in the head.
He only gets tenderness when he's
                    dead.

(Yevgeny Yevtushenko, 1955)

УТРЕННЯЯ ПОЧТА ДЛЯ А.А. АХМАТОВОЙ ИЗ ГОРОДА СЕСТРОРЕЦКА

В кустах Финляндии бессмертной,
где сосны царствуют сурово,
я полон радости несметной,
когда залив и Комарово
освещены зарей прекрасной,
осенены листвой беспечной,
любовью Вашей – ежечасной
и Вашей добротою – вечной.

(Иосиф Бродский, 1962)

НА СТОЛЕТИЕ АННЫ АХМАТОВОЙ

Страницу и огонь, зерно и жернова,
секиры острие и усеченный волос –
Бог сохраняет все; особенно – слова
прощенья и любви, как собственный свой голос.

В них бьется рваный пульс, в них слышен костный хруст,
и заступ в них стучит; ровны и глуховаты,
затем что жизнь – одна, они из смертных уст
звучат отчетливей, чем из надмирной ваты.

Великая душа, поклон через моря
за то, что их нашла, – тебе и части тленной,
что спит в родной земле, тебе благодаря
обретшей речи дар в глухонемой вселенной.

(Иосиф Бродский, 1989)

MORNING POST FOR A. A AKHMATOVA
FROM THE TOWN OF SESTRORETSK

In Finland's timeless forest verdure
which the tall dark pines reign over
I am filled with boundless rapture
when the bay and Komarovo
are lit with daybreak's radiant glory
and a careless leaf is falling,
your love's endlessly replenished store,
your goodness, timeless too, recalling.

(Joseph Brodsky, 1962)

ON THE CENTENARY OF ANNA AKHMATOVA'S BIRTH

The page and the fire, the millstone, the grain,
the blade of the axe, the hacked crop of hair –
God cares much for these, yet, as were they his own,
for two words – Love, Forgiveness – still fonder's his care.

In them beats a broken pulse, cracking of bones,
the knock of the spade; and even-paced, soft
(since life comes once only), more clear ring their tones
from the dead's mouths than from soundproofed heavens aloft.

Great soul, over oceans my reverence I'm sending
for finding them for us; to you, your remains
in our native soil sleeping, I give thanks for finding
the blest gift of speech in earth's deaf-mute domains.

(Joseph Brodsky, July 1989)

НАС ЧЕТВЕРО
Комаровские наброски

> *Ужели и гитане гибкой*
> *Все муки Данта сужены.* (О.М.)
>
> *Таким я вижу облик Ваш и взглад* (Б.П.)
>
> *О, Муза, Муза...* (М.Ц.)

...И отступилась я здесь от всего,
От земного всякого блага.
Духом, хранителем "места сего"
Стала лесная коряга.

Все мы немного у жизни в гостях,
Жить – это только привычка.
Чудится мне на воздушных путях
Двух голосов перекличка.

Двух? А еще у восточной стены,
В зарослях крепкой малины,
Темная, свежая ветвь бузины...
Это – письмо от Марины.

(Анна Ахматова, 1961)

130

FOUR OF US
Komarovskian Sketches

> *It may be that this slender gypsy woman*
> *is destined for all the pains of Dante's Hell...* (Ossip Mandelstam)
>
> *That's how I see your gaze, and see your profile* (B. Pasternak)
>
> *O, Muse, Muse...* (M. Tsvetaeva)

When I came here I gave up everything,
all those blessings earth provides.
My spirit, guardian of its domain,
became a tree-stump in the woods.

We're all like visitors in life:
living's a habit, nothing more.
But on the air I sense a stirring –
two voices calling back and fore.

Just two? – See, by the eastern wall,
dark, fresh, pushing out between a
clump of raspberry canes, a small
elder branch: a message from Marina.

(Anna Akhmatova, 1961)

[Б. Ахмадулиной Б. Мессереру]

Я пришел к поэту в гости,
вот и не застал поэта.
На веранде мяч и грозди
рассупоненной сирени.
Майский вечер. Воскресенье.
Черный пудель заперт в доме,
он глядит в окно покорно,
кроме пуделя и кроме
гостя, все вокруг спокойно –
темной зелени громада,
два пружинных акробата,
что забыты на скамейке
неприкаянного сада.
Я усядусь между ними,
погляжу вокруг покорно,
повторю за остальными:
"Все спокойно, все спокойно!"
Где поэт и где художник
этой ночью пропадают?
Да и сам я полуночник…

Этой ночью опадают
гроздья вохкие сирени
на скамейки, на колени
незадачливого гостя,
и, должно быть, очень просто
вас дождаться этой ночью.
Сумерки идут на убыль,
ты зачем отводишь очи,
черный просвещенный пудель?

(Евгений Рейн, 1982)

132

[To Bella Akhmadulina and K. Messerer]

I've come to visit the poet, but
she doesn't seem to be at home.
On the veranda: a ball, and a lot
of fallen lilac blossom. May,
late in the evening, and a Sunday.
A small black poodle, locked indoors,
stares, submissive, through the panes.
Except for dog and visitor
all round an utter stillness reigns
across the shady mass of green.
Two clockwork acrobats have been
forgotten, left upon a bench
that stands on the deserted lawn.
I sit between them, stare around
the place, submissive, and repeat
as if to these two left behind,
"It's quite alright, it's quite alright..."
Where have the poet and the painter
vanished to tonight? I thought
that I was the nocturnal creature!

With the passing of the night
more of these lilac blooms will drop
onto the bench, onto the lap
of this unlucky visitor,
who thinks, it won't be long for sure:
you're bound to come eventually...
Dawn can't be far. Dark starts to dwindle.
Why won't you look me in the eye,
you black, sophisticated poodle?

(Yevgeny Reyn, 1982)

THE WEB OF RELATIONSHIPS –
WHO WROTE ON WHOM?

Author of poem ⟶ Subject of poem

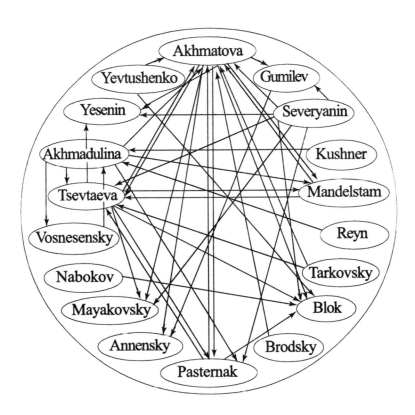

135

BELLA AKHMADULINA (b. 1937) reflects the new movement towards a personal poetic expression and a new lyricism that finally became possible, little by little, in the so-called 'thaw' that followed Stalin's death. The influence of the Acmeist poets, and especially of Akhmatova, is apparent in much of her work, which is clear and precise in form and imagery, often dealing with personal encounters or connections, or with everyday objects such as a motor-scooter or a gramophone. She was married first to Yevtushenko, and later to the novelist Nagibin.

ANNA AKHMATOVA (1889-1966) is one of the great poets of the twentieth century and her work is known the world over. In her verse, a classical purity and simplicity of form together with a clear, accurate vision are a vessel for profoundly felt emotions – in particular those associated with love, loss and suffering. She was married to Gumilev from 1910 to 1918, and the two of them, together with Mandelstam, formed the core of the Acmeist movement. At a time when many other writers went into exile, she chose to stay, and suffered accordingly. She saw many of those close to her executed (including Gumilev) or incarcerated (including her only son), while others committed suicide or died in appalling circumstances (Mayakovsky, Mandelstam). Furthermore, she saw her own work increasingly mocked and belittled, until finally she was expelled from the Writers' Union. Her poems are mostly small in scale, typically 12 or 16 lines, though later in her life she turned to longer forms, notably in the Requiem and 'Poem Without a Hero'.

INNOKENTY ANNENSKY (1856-1909), poet and extensive translator (including works by Euripides, Heine, Baudelaire, Verlaine and Rimbaud), was director of the Gymnasium in Tsarsky Selo, at which the young Akhmatova was a pupil, as was also her husband-to-be and fellow pupil Gumilev. His poetry was seen by the Acmeists as a step away from Symbolism and towards their own ideals.

137

ALEXANDER BLOK (1880-1921) is considered to be the greatest of the Russian Symbolist poets. His earlier poems dealt with love as a mystical process, and an unattainable ideal referred to as the 'Beautiful Lady', but the ethereally-lit atmosphere of these verses soon gave way to a much darker kind of imagery, full of emotional power and almost apocalyptic vision. As the Revolution approached he heralded it, notably in his most famous poem 'The Twelve', as a unique chance for a spiritual rebirth in Russia, but great disillusion was to follow, and he died in 1921, having written little in his last years. He was greatly revered and respected both by his contemporaries and the ensuing generations of poets, as the numerous poems to him in this book show.

JOSEPH BRODSKY (1940-1996) left school at 15 and for seven years worked in factories and various other short-term jobs, while continuing to educate himself. His first poetic ventures were too outspoken for the Soviet authorities and, after a notorious secret trial in 1964, he was convicted of 'parasitism' and sentenced to five years hard labour in the village of Norinskaya in the Arkhangelsk region. Fortunately, this was reduced to one-and-a-half years after an angry protest by Jean-Paul Sartre. In 1972 he was forced to leave the Soviet Union. He settled in the USA, and much of his later work was written in English. No further work of Brodsky's appeared in Russia till 1987, when the journal *новый мир* (*Novy Mir*) published a selection of his poems.

NIKOLAI GUMILEV (1880-1921) was one of the founders of the Acmeist group, and probably the most gifted poet of that movement after Akhmatova and Mandelstam. He studied in St. Petersburg and Paris, and travelled widely during his rather brief adult life, notably in Somalia and Ethiopia. He was a soldier in the First World War, and was decorated for bravery. With the end of the war came also his divorce from Akhmatova. He had married her in 1910 when she was barely out of her teens, but almost from the beginning they had begun to drift apart. He returned to live in Russia in 1918, but three years later he was arrested on suspicion of treason and shot.

138

The poetry of ALEXANDER KUSHNER (b. 1936), like that of Akhmadulina, signalled the return to a more intimate and personal mode of expression and subject matter in the post-Stalin years, and Brodsky considered him one of Russia's best twentieth-century lyric poets. Writing out of an urban context, he retains a classical attitude to form and is close in many ways to the Acmeists, as if taking up the pen where they left off. In 1999, Kushner was awarded the Pushkin Prize.

OSIP MANDELSTAM (1892-1938) is considered by many to be one of the greatest Russian poets of the last century, and by some, such as the poet Paul Celan, to be one of the greatest poets of all. He too was one of the Acmeists. His three volumes of poetry – *Stone*, *Tristia*, and *Poems* – reveal a strong connection with the works and values of Classicism (the title of his second book is also that of one of Ovid's works), and the forms he uses are essentially traditional. Yet his work is anything but archaic, often fusing widely-separated times and places in complex layers of startlingly luminous imagery, and his themes range from deep probings into the meaning and process of poetry to celebrations of such technological advances as the cinema and ice-cream. But in 1934 a poem ridiculing Stalin earned him exile, first to the Urals and then to Voronezh. He died in a labour camp near Vladivostok in 1938.

VLADIMIR MAYAKOVSKY (1893-1930) was the most gifted and outspoken of the Futurist poets. Breaking away from traditional forms, he developed a new poetic language of his own, powerfully driven by its punched-out stresses and colloquialisms, and characterised on the page by its 'stepped' layout. He was fiercely political, and is best-known for his 'thundering battle-calls', as Akhmatova terms his pro-revolution poetry. Yet as the '20s progressed and he saw the disastrous way things were going, he became bitterly disillusioned, and in 1930 he shot himself. Typically, the Stalinist regime subsequently exploited his work as it suited them and he was elevated to legendary status. Beneath the brash and charismatic exterior, however, lay an acutely vulnerable individual, unlucky in love and beset by loneliness. Yevtushenko's poem 'Tenderness' speaks of this side of his character.

VLADIMIR NABOKOV (1899-1977) and **BORIS PASTERNAK** (1890-1960) are both so well-known to the public at large – if only through the scandal over *Lolita* and David Lean's blockbuster film of *Doctor Zhivago* – that they need little introduction here. Nabokov left Russia at the onset of the Revolution, studied in Cambridge and, from 1922 till 1940, lived in Berlin. He finally settled in the United States. He is, of course, best known as a novelist, but also wrote a small amount of poetry.

Pasternak, on the other hand, made a name for himself first and foremost as a poet, the publication a few years after the revolution of the collection *My Sister Life* bringing him fame equalled only by Mayakovsky. *Zhivago*, unpublishable in the Soviet Union, came out eventually in an Italian edition and brought him the Nobel Prize. But his prose output was relatively small, and itself strongly infused with the poetry that formed the core of his work.

YEVGENY REYN (b. 1935) was born in St. Petersburg, and knew Akhmatova in her later years. He trained, and briefly worked, as a geologist, but then moved into journalism, and also wrote film scripts and children's books. His work has a quiet, descriptive quality, described by his close friend Brodsky, who used to refer to him as his 'teacher', as 'elegiac'. Thanks to the censors, Reyn's poetry did not appear in print in the Soviet Union until 1984, but has since become increasingly well-known both in Russia and, in recent years, also in the West, where translations have gradually appeared.

IGOR SEVERYANIN (1887-1941), on the other hand, is almost unknown in the West, probably due at least in part to the difficulties the translation of his work presents. Yet in Russia he is considered an important, though controversial, figure. He was well-thought of by his gifted contemporaries and, at a gathering in Moscow in 1918, he was crowned 'King of the poets', leaving Mayakovsky in second place. But he didn't appear to reciprocate such respect, for in 1934 he published *Medallions*, a set of 100 sonnets dedicated to individual poets and composers, the tone of which ranges from a certain degree of respect to mockery, sarcasm and downright derision. All the examples in this book are from this collection. Tsvetaeva called him 'a poet graced by God', but his poem to her is particularly vicious, and Pasternak fares little better. Severyanin led the splinter-group known as the Ego-Futurists.

ARSENY TARKOVSKY (1907-1989) was mainly known as a translator of poetry until, in his mid-fifties, he published his own first collection. But his work became well-known over the following two decades, above all through his son, the celebrated movie director Andrey Tarkovsky, who used recitations of Arseny's verse in several of his films. But though a 'late bloomer', he is ranked by some as one of the finest poets of the period, with strong links to those of the earlier part of the century. Indeed, he was one of the coffin-bearers at Akhmatova's funeral, along with Brodsky and the dead poet's son Lev, and he spoke the final words over her grave.

MARINA TSVETAEVA (1892-1941) is another of the great Russian poets of the first half of the century, though widespread recognition abroad has only come in more recent years, at least in part because she can be very difficult to translate effectively. Her voice is highly individual, and her work full of angular, rhythmic vigour and an almost physical feeling for sound, and liberally laced with exclamation marks and dashes. Born in Moscow, she spent much of her life in impoverished exile in Berlin, Paris and Prague. In 1939 she returned to Russia with her husband and daughter: he had been fighting on the side of the White Army in the past and was promptly arrested, while she herself was exiled to Yelabuga, where she hanged herself in 1941. Her first work was published in 1911, and she was one of the few poets of the time whose name is not associated with any particular group or movement. She had short but intense relationships – though mostly at a

141

distance, through letters – with Pasternak, Mandelstam and Rilke.

ANDREI VOZNESENSKY (b. 1933) is an almost exact contemporary of Yevtushenko, with whom he shares many characteristics. The roots of both reach back to Mayakovsky's politically-orientated poetry, and both struggled to remain in favour with, and loyal to, the regime and its principles, but at the same time maintaining their right to speak out in a society where freedom of speech and expression was still much restricted. His poems often have scientific or science-based titles and themes, ranging from nuclear power stations and motorbike races to airports and casinos.

SERGEI YESENIN (1895-1925) was born in a small village in Ryazan, but spent his youth in Moscow and then in St. Petersburg, where Blok introduced him to the literary scene. Yet the countryside and the rural life of his childhood lie at the heart of all his work, and he has been called 'the last of the peasant poets'. After a period of religious fervour and visions of a coming Utopia, he turned to a life of decadence and drink, and scandalised society with his affairs, including his marriage to the dancer Isadora Duncan, eighteen years his senior. However, in spite of his wild ways – he was commonly referred to as 'the hooligan' – he led a troubled inner life, which he ended in 1925 when he hanged himself in the Angleterre Hotel in St. Petersburg, having written a final farewell poem in his own blood. His verse is simple in form but his use of metaphor and imagery is quite striking and unusual and shows a deep understanding of language and its many levels.

YEVGENY YEVTUSHENKO (b. 1933) was one of the first, and probably most important, poets of the period immediately after Stalin's death. He burst onto the scene like a second Mayakovsky and, like Mayakovsky, he was a striking and powerful performer, often declaiming his works to huge gatherings. He swiftly gained, in a way that in the West is reserved for pop stars, a large following, for such freshness, energy, honesty and optimism had a great impact after years of Stalinist repression. Yet for a while he was criticised for what was seen as his support for the Soviet *status quo*, and writers such as Kingsley Amis accused him of condoning the invasion of Czechoslovakia and refusing to defend Pasternak in the latter's Nobel Prize controversy. But the accusations were based mainly on newspaper gossip, and he was not afraid to speak his mind, as in his famous 'Babi Yar', a poem about the mass murder of Jews in the concentration camp of that name. His poetry ranges from the lyrical to the political. Yevtushenko has travelled widely, and now lives in New York.

pp. 12-13 Written in 1914, shortly after Akhmatova had visited Blok.

pp. 14-15 The first in a set of sixteen poems by Tsvetaeva to Blok, to whom she bore a lifelong reverence, though she did not know him personally, and met him only briefly at one or two readings in Moscow in 1920.

pp. 16-17 Blok's response to Akhmatova's visit in 1914 – see above.

pp. 18-19 Daryal's Gorge is in Georgia, where Pasternak was living in the repressive 1930s, and is famous for its black rock.

pp. 20-21 In the early 1920s a close relationship existed between Tsvetaeva, living in Berlin, and Pasternak in Moscow. They exchanged some two hundred letters, and gave readings of one another's work. Such long distance involvements are characteristic of Tsvetaeva, who seemed to prefer the ideal, unfulfilled in reality, to the physical presence. Similar relationships, passionate on paper, would later develop with Osip Mandelstam and Rilke.

pp. 22-25 Tsvetaeva had already written a cycle of eleven poems to Akhmatova in 1916. Her love for Akhmatova's work, with which she had become acquainted as early as 1912, was deep and long-lasting. The two only met, however, in 1941, shortly before Tsvetaeva's suicide. The two men referred to in vss. 4 and 5 are presumably Blok, who died in 1921, and Gumilev (Akhmatova's first husband), executed in 1918.

pp. 26-27 Akhmatova's response to the foregoing poem by Tsvetaeva, written many years later, and only months before the latter's death.

pp. 28-29 The virtuosity of the word-play and the abundance of internal rhyme and syllable repetition make this poem extremely hard to render in English. I was able to use the prefix *dis-* for the Russian *ras-*, but the richness and musicality are quite impossible to reproduce.

pp. 30-31 "Blok was part of my youth… he had all the qualities which go to make a great poet – passion, gentleness, dedicated insight, his own conception of the world, his own gift of transforming everything he touched, his own reserved, restrained, self-effacing destiny." Thus Pasternak wrote in 1956. Yet he only met Blok once, in Moscow in May 1921, shortly before Blok's death. The present poem is from a set of four, entitled 'The Wind'.

pp. 36-39 Mandelstam made no secret of the fact that he had a sweet tooth, and one of his best-known poems is called 'Ice-cream'. In this poem, Akhmadulina makes the stark contrast between such freely-enjoyed sweetness and the misery of his later years of confinement and poverty.

pp. 40-41 It's interesting to compare Mandelstam's short verse on Akhmatova with Blok's, with which it shows similarities in both mood and imagery. *Rachel* was the stage name of actress Elisa Félix (1820-1852).

pp. 42-43 Voronezh: the town / province some 300 miles south of Moscow where Mandelstam lived in exile from 1934. The name is related to the Russian word for 'crow' (*voron*) – see line 5. Akhmatova visited him there in 1936.

pp. 44-45 Mandelstam visited Tsvetaeva in Moscow in January and February of 1916. Their short relationship was broken off when he left later that year. The poem's blending of apparently disconnected cities is typical of Mandelstam, yet not, however, random: 'Florence' (*flor* Lat. = flower) is also Tsvetaeva (*tsvet* Russ. = flower), and the Acropolis suggests the classical form and purity which he strove to integrate into Russian literature. Uspenski: the Cathedral of the Ascension in Moscow.

pp. 46-47 One of a set of eleven written to Mandelstam after his departure, the poem is a clear reflection of Tsvetaeva's preference for 'relationships at a distance' rather than physical proximity. She had similar liaisons with Pasternak and Rilke.

pp. 48-49 Besides this poem from 1921, Tsvetaeva wrote a set of seven others to Mayakovsky after his suicide in 1930.

pp. 50-1 / 52-3 These two sonnets are from the cycle *Medallions*, as are the other examples by Severyanin in this book. Pasternak receives particularly contemptuous treatment here, while Mayakovsky draws a certain grudging admiration.

pp. 54-57 This poem is very hard to translate in such a way that can convey all its implications. With its almost hermetic imagery and its complex layers of metaphor, Pasternak paints an intimate and luminous portrait of Akhmatova, but obliquely – skipping from one unusual image to the next, as if glimpsed in a dream. The 'column of salt' in the penultimate stanza refers to Akhmatova's poem 'Lot's wife' (1922-24).

pp. 58-9 / 60-1 These two poems, both on Annensky, are separated from one another by a long stretch of time, and reflect the importance that Akhmatova's teacher must have had on her in her early life. The first was written in 1911, two years after Annensky's death, and the second is a retrospective contemplation written thirty-five years later.

pp. 62-69 This fine ballad-like poem by Yevtushenko typifies the respect and reverence the young post-Stalin generation of poets held for Akhmatova, and was written in 1966 shortly after her death earlier in the same year.

pp. 70-71 Akhmatova wrote this poem in retrospect, some twenty-five years after its subject's death.

pp. 72-83 Mayakovsky wrote this vehement expression of his anger at the pointlessness of Yesenin's suicide shortly after that tragedy in the same year of 1925. Yet he, too, was to put an end to his own life a few years later.

A few references may need explaining: *Doronin* – Ivan Doronin (b. 1900) was a contemporary of Mayakovsky whose long epic poem 'The Tractor Driver' was criticised by Mayakovsky. The 'Angleterre' is the hotel where Yesenin hanged himself. *Sobinov* – Leonid von Sobinov sang the Tchaikovsky song 'Not a word, my friend' at a memorial meeting for Yesenin, and was well-known for his role as Lohengrin. *Kogan* – Piotr S.

147

Kogan was a literary critic / historian of the time.

pp. 84-85 While there is not only angry indignation but also grieving in Mayakovsky's lengthy polemic on Yesenin, Severyanin's sonnet is a cynical – though not wholly inaccurate! – caricature of the poet's life. Although dating from the same year, I haven't been able to discover whether it was written before or after Yesenin's death.

pp. 88-89 Yelabuga is the town near Chistapol in the Tatar Republic to which Tsvetaeva was evacuated in 1941 and where, ten days after her arrival, she hanged herself.

pp. 92-93 I haven't been able to trace the line by Akhmatova referred to here.

pp. 94-95 Both poems are to Akhmatova's husband and fellow-poet Nikolai Gumilev. The marriage was the culmination of a relationship begun while they were still at school, but was not destined to last very long, a fact that the dissatisfaction and disappointment expressed in these verses foreshadows.

pp. 96-99 Like Akhmatova, Gumilev was a pupil at Annensky's gymnasium.

pp. 100-101 This further sonnet from *Medallions* is principally a clever collage of titles of – or references to the titles of – books by Gumilev. The include the collections *The way of the conquistador, Romantic flowers, Pearls, The camp fire, The tent, The pillar of flame, African night, African hunt*. Gumilev made numerous journeys to Africa, as researcher, big-game hunter and adventurer, in the first decade or so of the century.

pp. 106-107 Michail A. Vrubel (1856-1910) was one the foremost Modernist painters of the time. 'The unknown woman' is the title of both a poem and a drama by Blok.

pp. 110-111 Another compilation of a poet's book-titles – included are: Akhmatova's first volume *Evening, Rosary*, and *White flocks*.

pp. 112-113 See note on Severyanin on p. 136.

pp. 114-117 Both poems by Tarkovsky are 'requiems': the first written shortly after the death of Tsvetaeva in 1941, the second nearly thirty years later and two years after the death of Akhmatova, at whose funeral he was present.

pp. 118-121 Marina Tsvetaeva's mother had been heading for a career as a concert pianist until her own domineering father cut it short and married her off. Marina learnt the instrument too for a while. *Gedike* is Alexander Gedike (sometimes written Goedicke), b. Moscow 1877, professor at the Moscow Conservatory – a pianist and composer whose works include a set of well-known and still-used studies.

pp. 122-123 Like 'The Unknown Woman' (see Severyanin's poem on Blok on pp. 106-7), 'The Fair Woman' refers to an eponymous poem of Blok's and represents the unattainable feminine ideal, Goethe's 'das ewig Weibliche'.

pp. 124-125 Just as Mayakovsky had lamented the reasons for Yesenin's suicide, so here does Yevtushenko in turn do the same for Mayakovsky, though in a much briefer way. The relation of the two poems to one another is clear, especially in the final couplets of each, both of which loosely paraphrase the same lines from Yesenin's suicide note.

pp. 126-127 Komarovo lies on the north coast of the Gulf of Finland, not far from St. Petersburg, and the Writer's Union had a small *dacha* there for the use of writers. Akhmatova spent much time there, and Sestroretsk, from where Brodsky sends his poem, lies across the bay a little further still to the west. Brodsky visited Akhmatova, accompanied and introduced by Reyn, in Komarovo in 1962.

pp. 128-129 There's a strong sense of transience in this late poem in which Akhmatova summons the spirits of Pasternak, Mandelstam and Tsvetaeva from her summer-house near Komarovo.

pp. 130-131 This poem by Reyn both concludes the cycle and returns to the beginning, being a light-hearted parody of the poem by Akhmatova to Blok which opens the collection.

PETER ORAM was born in Cardiff in 1947. He has first class honour degrees in Modern Languages (Cardiff) and Music (Aberystwyth) and an M.Mus in composition.

His publications include the novels *Maddocks* (Gomer Press, 1998), and *The Rub (Starborn* Books, 2001), the collection of poems *White* (Starborn Books, 2001) and several books of verse and music for education use. His poems and short stories have appeared in numerous magazines and anthologies.

In 2004, he composed the music for Alex Barr's musical *Swarm Fever* which received its first performance in the same year, since when he has been working on a second musical and further translations of Russian and German poetry.

Peter Oram has lived in London, in Spain and, for many years, in Pembrokeshire, but since 2001, has been living in Southern Germany.

Also available in the Arc Publications
TRANSLATION series
(Translations Editor: Jean Boase-Beier)

ROSE AUSLÄNDER (Germany)
Mother Tongue: Selected Poems
Translated by Jean Boase-Beier & Anthony Vivis

*A Fine Line: New Poetry from Eastern
& Central Europe* (anthology)
EDS. JEAN BOASE-BEIER, ALEXANDRA BÜCHLER, FIONA SAMPSON
Various translators

FRANCO FORTINI (Italy)
Poems
Translated by Michael Hamburger

EVA LIPSKA (Poland)
Pet Shops & Other Poems
Translated by Basia Bogoczek & Tony Howard

Altered State: An Anthology of New Polish Poetry
EDS. ROD MENGHAM, TADEUSZ PIÓRO, PIOTR SZYMOR
Translated by Rod Mengham, Tadeusz Pióro *et al*

CATHAL Ó SEARCAIGH (Ireland)
By the Hearth in Mín a' Leá
Translated by Frank Sewell, Seamus Heaney & Denise Blake

TOMAZ SALAMUN (Slovenia)
Homage to Hat, Uncle Guido and Eliot
Translated by the author, Charles Simic, Anselm Hollo,
Michael Waltuch *et al*
Row
Translated by Joshua Beckman and the author

GEORG TRAKL (Austria)
To the Silenced: Selected Poems
Selected, introduced and translated by Will Stone

Six Slovenian Poets (anthology)
ED. BRANE MOZETIČ
Translated by Anna Jelnikar, Kelly Lennox Allen & Stephen Watts